Quick and Fun Games for Preschoolers

Annette EC Guerrero

Teacher Created Materials, Inc.

Illustrated by Jethro Wall

Cover Design by Chris Macabitas

Made in U.S.A.

ISBN 1-57690-366-4

Order Number TCM 2366

Table of Contents

Introduction

Your preschooler has the energy to run circles around you. Let him. Let him hop, skip, and jump, too. Channel his energies into learning. Get his whole body involved in understanding the basic concepts he will need as he enters the world of schooling.

Some children are good visual learners, some are good auditory learners, and some are better kinesthetic (physical) learners. But children learn their best when you teach a concept involving all three of these areas of learning. Your child sees it, he says it, and he does it. In at least three different ways, his brain is picking up the concept that is being taught.

The games in this book have been developed to get your preschooler moving, learning, and having fun.

The time you spend teaching your child will be special and well spent. Always encourage your child and praise him often. Shower him with lots of hugs.

How to Use This Book

The games in this book are meant to be simple. The materials are ordinary and easily adapted. If you don't have a foam ball, use an old rolled-up sock, instead. With chalk and cheap masking tape, you already have the major materials needed for more than half the games.

Remember, you know your child better than anyone. You know his capabilities. If he already knows his uppercase letters, make the necessary adjustments and have the game teach lowercase letters. Many of the variations on each game offer suggestions to expand your child's learning. Feel free to come up with your own variations that meet your child's needs.

Play a game for a week. You can play the game again, in a few weeks, to reinforce or reteach a concept. These games can be enjoyed over and over again.

Keep the games moving and fast paced. Sometimes your child will want to play the game for just a few minutes and sometimes for an hour. Let him explore. Let him learn. And listen to his own variation on the game. Several games in this book are just that, a child's own variation on a game. Leave the games set up for a while. A masking tape clock won't hurt your carpeting for a week (and it makes a great conversation piece with company). Every time your child sits down and becomes an hour hand, he is getting closer to understanding telling time.

Above all, make it fun. Children have such a great desire to learn and they love to play. You can help them realize that learning can be fun.

Indoor Games

Indoor Games *(cont.)*

Hallway Hop

Your child will get a jump on his counting skills each time he hops down the hallway.

Materials:

- masking tape
- ruler
- any hallway

Directions

Use any hallway that your child uses frequently. The hallway to his bedroom or the bathroom is always a good one. Create a square on the floor at one end of the hallway using four strips of masking tape ten inches (25 cm) long. Place your next tape square six inches (15 cm) away from your first square. Make ten squares. Create a tape number in each square starting with the number 1. Your child starts by hopping into the number 1 square with both feet and calling out "one." He continues hopping into each square calling out its number until he reaches the end of the hallway. Then he returns by hopping into the number 10 square and counting backwards until he reaches the first square. Encourage your child to hop down the hallway every time he needs to go through it. Soon counting to ten will be a breeze.

Variations:

- Use the uppercase and lowercase letters of the alphabet.

- Start with a number other than one, such as seven or ten.

- Count by 2's, 5's, or 10's.

What's Your Number?

It is always important that your child knows her home phone number.

Materials:

- masking tape
- yardstick
- index cards
- markers

Directions

As large as you can, write each digit of your phone number on a separate index card. With the masking tape, create seven squares on your living room floor. Make each box 12 inches (30 cm) on each side. Line them up in a row as if you were writing your phone number.

| 3 | 8 | 2 | – | 1 | 4 | 6 | 3 |

Make three squares, make a dash, and make four more squares. Start with the first digit in your phone number. Place the index card with that number in the first box. Have your child jump into the first square and call out the number. Then have your child step out of the square. Place the index card with the next digit of your phone number into the second square. Have your child hop into the first square, call out the number, hop into the second square, and call out that number. Again, your child steps out of the square and returns to the beginning. Repeat the process for the third digit in your phone number. You may want to have your child hop through the three-number sequence several times before starting with the fourth digit. Continue the same process with the rest of the digits of your phone number. Once this is done, flip the first index card over so your child can't see the number and then have her hop through the number sequence again. Continue until all of the index cards are flipped over and your child has memorized her phone number.

Boxcars

Materials:

- five boxes
  (can be the
  size of a
  shoebox or a
  little bigger)
- stuffed
  animals

With a train of boxes, your child is in first place.

Directions

Line the boxes up in your living room as if they were the boxcars of a train. Next, have your child collect ten of his favorite stuffed animals. Have him choose one animal (a big teddy bear works well) to be the engineer. Place the animal in front of the box on the left, facing forward. Explain to your child that the box on the far left is the front of the train, and therefore, is the first boxcar. The box to the far right is the last boxcar. Then start loading the boxcars. Tell your child to put his brown teddy bear in the first boxcar. He should place his bear in the box on the far left. Make sure he places the stuffed animals facing forward, like the engineer, to give your child the impression that the train of cars is moving forward toward the left. Have him put two more stuffed animals in the fourth boxcar. He should count the boxes from the left, in order, to find the fourth car. Continue giving different directions using first, second, third, fourth and fifth as names for the boxcars.

Variation:

- Make it more challenging by giving more specifics in the directions such as, "Place the pink bunny behind the second boxcar" or "Put the orange cat in the boxcar in front of the fourth boxcar."

Stair Steppin'

Materials:

- paper
- markers
- masking tape
- stairs
- scissors
- ruler

Stepping up the steps, she counts forward. Stepping down, she counts backwards.

Directions

Cut 11 five-inch (13-cm) squares from the paper. Using the markers, write one number on each square starting with 0 and ending with 10. Starting at the bottom of the stairs, tape the 0 square to the left side of the step. Continue up the steps in numerical order. Have your child start at the bottom of the stairs. As she ascends each step, have her count the number out loud. When she reaches the top, have her turn around and descend the stairs while counting backwards. Encourage her to count every time she goes up or down the stairs.

Variations:

- Count by 2's, 5's, or 10's.
- Remove one or more of the paper numbers so she must fill in the blanks.
- Use different groups of numbers, for example, 11–20.
- Use the letters of the alphabet.

Special Square

Materials:

- about a dozen stuffed animals
- masking tape
- yardstick

Your child's favorite stuffed animals will help him sort through this game.

Directions

Create a three-foot (91 cm) square on the floor with the masking tape. Gather all the stuffed animal friends your child can find. Have him place the animals randomly around the room but not in the square. Tell your child that in order for an animal to get into the square, there must be something special about that animal. You will tell your child what that special thing is. For example, "The thing that makes your animal special is . . . he is a teddy bear." Your child will then collect all the teddy bears and put them into the special square. Other special characteristics might include having brown eyes, black fur, a tail, fins, teeth, or a pink nose. Start with easy attributes and then get more challenging. Have your child remove the animals from the square and start again. End the game with your child being the "animal" who gets to be in the special square.

Variation:

- Make the game more challenging by having two special features the animal must have before being able to go into the special square. For example, the animal must be a teddy bear with black fur.

Find My Match

Materials:

- matching pairs of household things

One shoe on the rug, another behind a chair, your child looks high and low to find all the matching pairs.

Directions

Collect ten identical pairs of household items. Scatter just one of each pair around your living room. They can be on furniture and under furniture, as long as part of the object is visible. Next, show your child the other half of the pair, let's say a red tennis shoe. Your child then searches the living room for its matching mate. Place the pair side by side on the floor, and then continue the game.

Possible Pairs:

- shoes, mittens, food cans, gloves, boxes of macaroni, pencils, pens, pillows, books, markers, construction paper shapes, pop cans, blocks, crayons, toy cars, toothbrushes, combs, hair brushes, balls, toy soldiers, video tapes, cassette tapes, rolls of masking tape, spoons, potholders, dish rags, hair bows, and Christmas bows

Variation:

- Hide all of the objects and have your child find the pairs.

Body Clock

Materials:

- masking tape
- strip of poster board, three feet by five inches (91 cm x 13 cm)
- scissors
- 12 paper plates
- markers
- measuring tape

Your child's whole body will know what time it is.

Directions

On the floor with the masking tape, create a circle eight feet (2.4 m) in diameter. In the center of the circle place a small X of tape. The strip of poster board will be the minute hand. To create the point of the minute hand, trim the corners on one end of the poster board starting five inches (13 cm) down on each side so that the cuts meet on the short side in the middle. Tape the poster board strip to the floor inside the circle. Place the straight edge at the center X and the point pointing toward the perimeter of the circle. Next, with the markers, number each paper plate with the numerals 1–12. Tape the number 12 paper plate above the point of the poster board, then tape the rest of the plates to the floor as if they were the numbers on a clock. Next, have your child sit in the center of the circle on the taped X with his legs together, sticking straight out. Your child's legs become the hour hand of the body clock. Discuss with your child how the minute hand and the hour hand move so that he knows that his legs will be the ones that tell the hours. You then call out a time, such as five o'clock. Your child then moves his legs to point to the five. He tells you that the minute hand is on the 12, the hour hand is on the five, and so it is five o'clock. Continue to call all the numbers randomly.

Variation:

- Point the poster board to the six and do half hour times.

Clothespin Addition

Materials:

- bucket
- 12 clothespins
- a red permanent marker
- a blue permanent marker
- masking tape
- measuring tape

A toss in the bucket and your child will be adding it all together.

Directions

Using the permanent markers, color six clothespins red and six clothespins blue. With the masking tape, make a line 18 inches (46 cm) long on the floor. Place the bucket five feet (1.5 m) from that line. Have your child stand behind the line and try tossing the clothespins, one at a time, into the bucket. When your child has tossed all of her clothespins, pick up the bucket and bring it back to the taped line. Leave the clothespins that did not make it into the bucket where they are on the floor. Have your child dump out the bucket on the line and sort the clothespins into two piles—red and blue. Have her count the red ones and then the blue ones. Then have her add the two groups of clothespins together. Say, "Three red clothespins and four blue clothespins made it into the bucket. Therefore, three plus four more gives us a total of seven." Encourage your child to verbalize the equation. Return the bucket, collect all the clothespins and start again.

Variations:

- Add more clothespins for more challenging addition problems.
- Make up story problems.
- Write the math equations on paper using a red marker and a blue marker. Use a black marker for the answer.

Dot-to-Dot

Materials:

- a dozen paper plates
- markers
- masking tape
- yarn or string

A life-sized dot-to-dot has your child counting.

Directions

Using the markers, write a number on each of the paper plates starting with 1 and ending with 12. The paper plates are the "dots." Tape the paper plates to the floor to create a shape. You can create a known shape like a square, circle, oval, triangle, rectangle, heart, star, diamond, or even a house. Or you or your child may create any shape you wish. Just make sure the numbers are in order. Securely tape one end of the yarn next to the number 1 paper plate. Then have your child "draw" a line to the number 2 plate, using the yarn. Either tape the yarn to the floor next to the plate or wrap the yarn around the outside of the paper plate. The tape holding the plate to the floor will hold the yarn if your child does not pull too hard. Remember that the last plate must be right next to the number 1 plate in order to finish the picture.

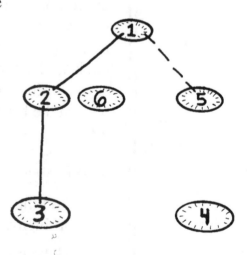

Variation:

- Use uppercase or lowercase letters as the "dots."

Out of Order

Materials:

- ten paper plates
- markers

Lining up her numbers is as easy as one, two, three.

Directions

Using the markers, write a number on each of the paper plates starting with 1 and ending with 10. Randomly lay the paper plates on the floor. As quickly as he can, have your child line up the paper plates in numerical order. Make it a race against time. Lay the plates out again and start over.

Variations:

- Have your child start with 10 and line up the numbers backwards.
- To make it simpler, use three plates to put in order, such as 5, 6, and 7.
- Create plates for the numerals 11 through 20 and then have your child put them in order.
- Use the letters of the alphabet.
- Include zero in the line up.

Puddle Splashing

Material:

- masking tape
- two paper bags
- string
- index cards
- markers
- yardstick

Splish, splash, and your child counts up a storm as she jumps from puddle to puddle in her boots.

Directions

Randomly create 12 "puddles" on the floor with the masking tape. Make the masking tape puddles 24 inches (61 cm) in diameter and 18 inches (46 cm) apart. Using the markers, write the numbers 1 through 12 on the index cards. Tape an index card inside each of the puddles. Have your child put the paper bags over her shoes. Using the string, tie the paper bags around her shins or ankles. Then have her start puddle jumping. She jumps into a masking tape puddle. Let's say the number in the puddle is five. Your child jumps five times, as high as she can, making five big imaginary splashes. She then continues splashing through the puddles.

Variations:

- Have your child splash through the puddles in numerical order.

- Have your child splash through the puddles counting backwards from 10.

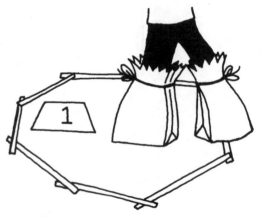

Petals

Material:

- construction paper
- scissors
- masking tape
- ruler

Flower petals become a mathematical learning experience.

Directions

Out of the construction paper, cut two circles six inches (15 cm) in diameter. Also cut 20 different colored flower petals eight inches (20 cm) in length. Tape the circles to the floor two feet (61 cm) apart. These are the centers of the flowers. Have your child place some petals around the flower center on the left. Then you place petals around the flower center on the right (decide whether you will have more or less petals than your child). Ask your child if your flower has more or less petals than his. Encourage him to say, "My flower has (more or less) petals than Mommy's flower." Clear away the petals and repeat the process.

Variations:

- Use greater than and less than. See the game, "Is It More? Is It Less?", on page 33.

- Use the petals for counting. You make up a flower and have your child count the petals. Have your child put the petals on the flower and then count them.

- Use the petals for adding one more. Have your child place a number of petals on the flower. Have him count them. Ask him how many petals he will have if he adds one more.

Teddy To Beddy

Materials:

- paper plates
- markers
- teddy bears
- a die

A trail of paper plates leads your child right to bed.

Directions

Starting at your child's bed, lay down a trail of paper plates that leads to the living room. Have your child choose her favorite teddy bear and place the bear at the beginning of the trail, which is the living room. Next, have your child toss the die. Whatever number comes up on the die, your child counts off that number of plates using her teddy bear. For instance, if your child rolls a three, her teddy bear hops three plates. She continues to roll the die again and moves her teddy bear along the paper plate trail. She must roll the exact number to be able to jump into bed.

Variation:

- Have the trail lead to the bathroom first, so your child can brush her teeth.

Equal?

Materials:

- masking tape
- groups of household objects or toys, such as spoons, straws, crayons, socks, mittens, shoes, plastic cups, plastic lids, blocks, toy soldiers, bows, plastic links, or toy cars
- a paper plate
- marker
- yardstick

Identifying sets as equal or not equal is as simple as flipping a paper plate.

Directions

Using the masking tape, create two circles two feet (61 cm) in diameter. Place them one foot (30 cm) apart. On one side of the paper plate, draw a large equal sign (=). On the other side of the paper plate draw a not equal sign (a = with a / through it). Next, have your child create a set in the masking tape circle on the left. Be sure your child understands that a set is a group of objects that are the same. Let's say he creates a set of five toy cars. In the circle on the right, you create a set. You make the set either equal or not equal. Let's say you create a set of four spoons. Your child then counts the sets and decides if they are equal or not equal. He then places the paper plate between the two circles to show the correct sign. In this case, he would show the sign that says the sets are not equal. Then have your child say, "My set of toy cars is not equal to your set of spoons." Start over with your child creating a new set.

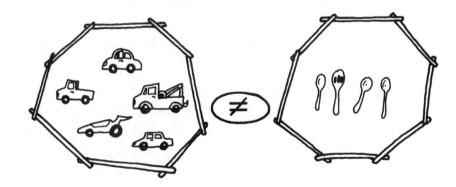

Grid Work

Materials:

- masking tape
- index cards
- markers
- favorite stuffed animals
- yardstick

Understanding how a grid works is as easy as placing a favorite toy in the right box.

Directions

Create a four by four-foot (120 cm x 120 cm) grid on the floor using masking tape. The grid will have a total of 16 squares, each measuring one-foot (30 cm) square. On four of the index cards, using the markers, write the numbers 1, 2, 3, and 4. Tape these cards above the grid in numerical order starting on the left. These are the numbers of the columns on the grid. On another four index cards write the letters A, B, C, and D. Tape these cards to the left of the grid starting at the top with card A. These are the letters of the rows on the grid. Therefore, the first box in the upper left-hand corner will have the label A-1. The box in the lower right-hand corner will have the label D-4. Before you begin the game, familiarize your child with how the grid works. For example, say, "Tommy Turtle's favorite place to sit is in box A-4." Your child

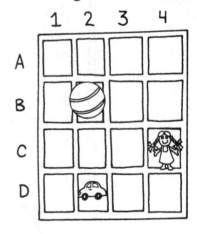

takes his toy turtle, finds row A, moves down to column 4, and places the toy in the square. Continue with the next stuffed toy until all of the squares are filled. Then have your child remove the animals in the same way.

Big Bingo

Materials:

- masking tape
- index cards
- markers
- yardstick
- a paper bag
- favorite stuffed animals

She finds the right boxes on a grid and BINGO! She's got it.

Directions

Create a four by four-foot (120 cm x 120 cm) grid on the floor using masking tape. The grid will have a total of 16 squares each measuring one-foot (30 cm) square. On four of the index cards, using the markers, write the numbers 1, 2, 3, and 4. Tape these cards above the grid in numerical order starting on the left. These are the numbers of the columns on the grid. On another four index cards write the letters A, B, C, and D. Tape these cards to the left of the grid starting at the top with card A. These are the letters of the rows on the gird. Therefore, the first box in the upper left-hand corner will have the label A-1. The box in the lower right-hand corner will have the label D-4. On sixteen index cards, write the labels for each box: A-1, A-2, A-3, A-4, B-1, B-2, B-3, B-4, C-1, C-2, C-3, C-4, D-1, D-2, D-3, and D-4. Place these 16 cards into the paper bag. Shake the bag. Have your child draw a card from the bag. She reads it, figures it out, and places a stuffed animal in that box. She lays the card off to the side of the grid and chooses another card out of the bag. She wins when she gets BINGO or four in a row vertically, horizontally, or diagonally.

The Run Around

Materials:

- 11 paper plates
- markers
- masking tape
- measuring tape

'Round and 'round he goes, and where he stops is on the number he knows.

Directions

On the floor, create a masking tape circle that is six feet (1.8 m) in diameter. Tape a one-foot (30-cm) line perpendicular to the circle. This will be the "starting" line. Write a number on each of the paper plates starting with the 0 and ending with 10. Randomly tape the paper plates inside the circle. Have your child stand behind the starting line. Say, "On your mark, get set, go find the number seven." Your child must run completely around the circle, return to the starting line, and then run and jump on the paper plate that has the number seven on it. Have him return to the starting line and continue with another number.

Variations:

- Use letters of the alphabet.
- Use shapes or colors.
- Use sets.

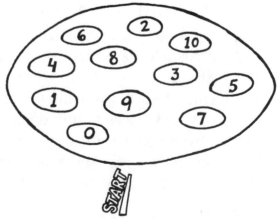

Musical Matching Hearts

Materials:

- construction paper
- wallpaper samples or leftovers
- ruler
- scissors
- a paper bag
- masking tape
- radio or tape/CD player

There's music, there's matching, and there's hearts. What more could your little love ask for?

Directions

Cut 20 six-inch (15 cm) hearts out of the construction paper and the wallpaper. They must all be different sizes. Next, cut the hearts in half from top to bottom. Tape the left half of each heart randomly on the floor. Put the right half of each heart into a paper bag. Start the music. Have your child choose one half of a heart from the paper bag. As the music continues to play, she studies the hearts taped to the floor, but she cannot move. When you stop the music, she runs to the half of a heart that matches hers and lays it down. She then returns to the paper bag and waits for you to start the music again.

Variation:

- Put some halves of hearts that have no match into the paper bag. When the music stops, your child hands you the half of a heart and says, "No match."

Step in Time

Materials:

- steps
- 12 paper plates
- markers
- masking tape

Your child will step right into telling time.

Directions

Using the paper plates and markers, make 12 clocks. Make each clock with its hands showing a different hour: one o'clock, two o'clock, three o'clock, and so on, up to twelve o'clock. Next, tape the plates to the stairs. Start with one o'clock on the first step, two o'clock on the second step, and so on until you reach the top step, which will be the twelve o'clock paper plate. Have your child start at the bottom of the steps. As he hops onto the first step, he calls out, "one o'clock." When he hops onto the second step, it's two o'clock. He continues this process all the way to the top of the stairs. Then call out the times randomly, and have him find the correct time on the stairs.

Variations:

- Create an extra paper plate clock with movable hands. You can use cardboard or construction paper for the hands and a brad to hold them together in the center of the plate. This time, as your child ascends the stairs, he must match his clock with the time on the paper plate taped to the stair.

- Using your child's clock with the movable hands, give him a time. Have him make his clock say that time, then he must find the matching time on the stairs.

Mitten Matching

Materials:

- wallpaper samples or scraps
- scissors
- yarn
- 14 clothespins
- two chairs

First find one mitten, then the other. Just like the good little kittens, your child will find all the mittens.

Directions

Cut seven pairs of mittens from different wallpaper scraps. Make them as large as you can. Be sure to have a variety of colors and patterns with no two pairs of mittens the same. Also, make sure you have a right mitten and a left mitten. Next, create a clothesline with the chairs and yarn. Set the chairs ten feet (2.5 m) apart. Tie the yarn to each of the chairs to make a clothesline. Hang the left mitten of each pair on the clothesline with the clothespin. Scatter the right hands of the pairs of mittens over the floor. When you say, "go," your child picks up a mitten from the floor and pins it by its match on the clothesline.

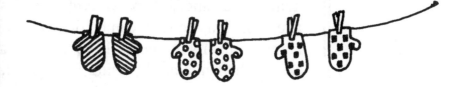

Variations:

- Place the mittens design-side down and have a game of memory. Flip over two mittens. If they match, your child keeps the pair. If they don't, your child flips them back over and turns over two more mittens.

- Use different colored construction paper.

Milky Way

Materials:

- different colored construction paper
- scissors
- masking tape ruler

The stars up above become part of the mathematical equation.

Directions

Cut out 25 stars from the construction paper. Make some of the stars two inches (5 cm) wide and some four inches (10 cm) wide. There does not have to be an equal number. Randomly tape stars to a door in your house. Start with an amount your child can count. Have your child guess or estimate (and be sure to use these words) how many stars are taped to the wall. Once your child makes her guess, she counts the stars. She does this by removing the stars from the door and taping them in a line on the floor. When they are all on the floor, have her count them one more time. Ask your child if this is the number she guessed (estimated). Ask her what her number was and if there were more or less stars than she guessed. This activity can be done every day, with a new number of stars to guess. If your child can count to 25 easily, challenge her by using 30 or 35 stars.

Variations:

- Sort the stars according to color after your child has counted them.
- Sort the stars according to size.

Beat, Beat, Beat Went My Heart

Materials:

- coffee can, potato chip can, ice cream bucket, or oatmeal container with a lid
- red construction paper hearts

Counting the beats of your heart is a game your child will love.

Directions

Cut out at least ten hearts. You can cut out more and use them to decorate the can. Have your child practice beating the can to relieve the temptation. Begin by tapping out a certain number of beats, let's say five. Give the drum to your child and he must tap out five beats, counting them as he does. Do this for all the numbers from one through ten. Then use the construction paper hearts to tell your child how many times to beat the drum. For example, lay out three hearts. He must beat the drum three times.

Variations:

- Have your child repeat different rhythm patterns.
- Have your child beat the drum at different speeds—fast, slow, in a continuous rhythm pattern, or irregularly.

Leaves Of Fall

Materials:

- brown, red, yellow, orange, and green construction paper
- scissors
- masking tape
- yardstick

Falling leaves equal subtraction facts.

Directions

Using the brown construction paper, cut out the trunk and bare branches of a tree. Make the tree 3 ¹/₂ feet (1 m) tall. Tape the tree to any door in your house. With the rest of the construction paper, make different shaped leaves eight inches (20 cm) long. Make a total of 10 leaves. Discuss with your child the attributes of the season of fall (autumn), such as the leaves changing color, the weather getting colder, and the leaves falling. Tape five leaves to the branches of the tree. Create story problems that deal with subtraction. For example, tell your child, "In my tree I have five leaves. The wind blew very hard and three leaves fell off my tree." Take three leaves off the top of the tree and place them at the foot of the tree. Ask your child, "How many leaves are left in the tree?" Have your child count the number of leaves that are left among the branches. Encourage her to answer, "There are two leaves left." Reply, "That's right. We started with five leaves, three fell off, and two were left. Five take away three is equal to two." Continue this process starting with any number of leaves up to a total of ten. Be sure to vary the explanation of how the leaves fell off the tree—a squirrel knocked them off, a caterpillar chewed their stems, Daddy climbed up in the tree and plucked them off.

Variations:

- Use more leaves.
- Write the math equations on paper.

Big Roller

Materials:

- a die
- six paper plates
- markers

A roll of the die, and sets come alive.

Directions

Make sets on your paper plates. You can use dots or circles or hearts. Just make sure all of the objects in the set are the same. One plate will have a set of one object drawn on it. Another plate will have a set of two objects drawn on it. Do this on all of the plates up to a set of six. Spread the plates out in a large circle in your living room. Have your child stand in the middle of the circle of plates and roll the die. Whatever number she rolls, she must run to the matching set drawn on the paper plate and count the  objects in that set. For example, if your child rolls a five, she must find the paper plate with the set of five hearts drawn on it and count to five. Then she returns to the center of the circle and rolls the die again.

Variations:

- Add another die and six more paper plates and have sets all the way up to 12.

- Make cards with the numbers 1 through 6 written on them. Lay them on the floor around your child's feet. When she rolls the die, she must pick up the matching number and place it on the set with the same number of objects.

Beanbag Equations

Materials:

- a beanbag
- paper plates
- beans (lima, navy, or pinto)
- masking tape
- large plastic bowl
- markers
- measuring tape

He tosses a beanbag, and it all adds up to a great equation for learning.

Directions

Using the markers, write the numbers 0 through 9 on the paper plates. Randomly tape the paper plates to the floor in an area five feet (1.5 m) wide and three feet (1 m) deep. Empty a bag of beans into a large plastic bowl. Make a tape line one foot away from the area of paper plates. Tape two plain paper plates next to each other on the floor three feet (1 m) away from where your child will stand. Your child starts by standing behind the line. He tosses the beanbag onto one of the paper plates. Say the beanbag lands on the paper plate with the number 5 on it. Your child then runs over to the bowl and removes five beans from it and places them on the plain paper plate on the left. He retrieves the beanbag and returns to stand behind the line. Again, he tosses the beanbag. Let's say it lands on the number 3 plate. Your child then runs to the bowl, grabs three beans, and places them on the plain paper plate on the right. Say, "You started with five beans. You added three more beans. How many beans do you have all together?" Have your child count up the beans. After your child answers, "eight," put the beans back in the bowl and start the game over again.

Shadow Shapes

Materials:

- newsprint or butcher paper
- markers
- household objects

Shadows take shape as your child matches the objects' mates.

Directions

Collect different household objects. You might include things like a wooden spoon, a glove, a plastic plate, a book, a shoe, or a plastic toy ring. Randomly trace an outline of each object on the newsprint. Place all the household objects in a pile on the floor next to the newsprint. Have your child find the traced shadows that match the real object, placing the real object over its "shadow." Your child can color the outlined figures after she has matched them all. Find a few new objects and start again.

Sardines

Materials:

- a gallon-sized freezer bag
- objects that you have a lot of (socks, blocks, balls, spoons, etc.)

Guess how many are in the bag. Let's count and find out.

Directions

Gather a group of objects that are the same, such as socks. Put as many socks as you can into a freezer bag and seal it. Have your child guess (estimate) how many socks are in the bag. Once he makes his guess, he opens the bag and counts the socks to see if he is correct. Ask him if the number he guessed is the same as the number he counted. Was it more or less?

Other Possible Items:

- plastic building bricks
- books
- small stuffed animals
- plastic lids
- plastic cups
- plastic bowls
- plastic plates
- crayons
- pennies
- checkers
- poker chips
- marshmallows
- gloves
- hats
- toy cars
- washcloths
- boxes of gelatin
- Christmas bows

Is It More? Is It Less?

Materials:

- masking tape
- groups of household objects (toy jewelry, plastic Easter eggs, scarves, buttons, poker chips, plastic plates, books, stuffed animals, wooden spoons, or hot pads)
- a paper plate
- marker
- yardstick

Does the set have more or less objects than the other? This is the question your child must answer.

Directions

Using the masking tape, create two circles two feet (61 cm) in diameter. Place the circles one foot (30 cm) apart. On the paper plate, draw a good-sized less than sign (<). The plate can be turned around to show a greater than sign (>). Have your child create a set in the left masking tape circle. Let's say your child creates a set of seven bracelets. Then you create a set in the right circle. You create a set that is either more or less than your child's set. Let's say you create a set of four buttons. Your child must then compare the two sets and decide if her set is more or less than your set. Remember, you must always read the sets from left to right. Your child then places the paper plate so that it forms a true sentence. In this case your child's set is greater than (>) your set. You can say, "The set of bracelets is greater than (>) the set of buttons. Be sure to say the words "greater than" and "less than." Clear the sets and start again.

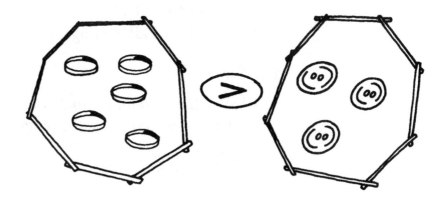

Straw Stretch

Materials:

- plastic straws (strips of construction paper or yarn pieces will do)
- scissors
- measuring tape

Lining up straws end-to-end gives your child an idea of length.

Directions

Cut the straws (construction paper or yarn pieces) into different lengths. Leave some straws their original length. Have your child leave the room so that you can hide the straws throughout the living room. When you are finished, have your child return. Tell him you will count aloud, slowly, to 25 as he gathers as many straw pieces as he can find. When you reach 25, tell him to stop. Next, have him lay the straws end-to-end across the living room floor. When he is done, he can measure his straws with the measuring tape. Hide the straws and start all over again.

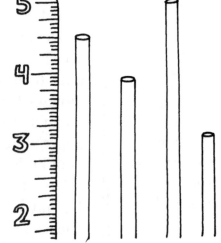

Variations:

- Change the amount of time your child has to gather the straws and compare the lengths.

Time to Tally

Materials:

- white paper
- pencil
- markers
- clipboard,
- household objects or toys

Your child will tally up anything and everything she can find.

Directions

Using a marker, divide a piece of white paper (the long way) into four columns. Draw an intersecting line on the left-hand side of the paper two inches (5 cm) from the end to make a row of four boxes. In those boxes, draw a picture of four things your child will be counting around the house (Possibilities might include doors, doorknobs, windows, beds, sinks, balls, people, animals, phones, drawers, lamps, or stairs). Insert the paper into the clipboard. Explain to your child how to tally objects when counting them. Make sure she understands to make groups of five by making four vertical lines and then a diagonal line for counting the fifth object. You may want to start with objects that only add up to numbers less than five and then move to objects up to ten. When you feel she understands the concept of tallying, send her off on her tally hunt around the house.

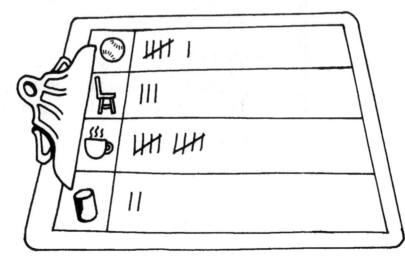

Find 10

Materials:

• none

Your child is counting to 10 as he goes on the hunt.

Directions

Your child has 10 fingers, and he will be using them to count 10 things in a category. Let's say your category is brown. Your child must hunt around the house for objects that are brown. He starts with both hands in fists. As he finds a brown object, such as a rug, he pops out one of his fingers. He goes to another room and finds his brown teddy bear and up comes another finger. He continues until all 10 of his fingers are sticking straight out. Have your child make two fists and start again.

Possible Categories:

• big things, small things, red things, shiny things, furry things, rough things, square things, round things, long things, things you sit on, things you sleep on, straight things, smooth things, soft things, fluffy things, things you hear, things that light up, things that open, warm things, cold things, and things you wear

Variations:

• If your child has trouble counting to 10, start with just five objects and five fingers.

Balloon Number Volley

Materials:

- yarn
- two chairs
- balloon
- measuring tape

Get a volley going, and your child will learn what number comes next.

Directions

Create a net using yarn and two chairs. Place the chairs six feet (2 m) apart and tie a strip of yarn between the two chairs. Blow up a balloon and tie it off. Have your child stand on one side of the net, and you stand on the other. You start by tossing the balloon over the net and calling out a number. Let's say you call out "five." Your child then hits the balloon back to you and calls out "six." You return it and call out "seven." Continue counting until the balloon is missed. Then start the game over with another number.

Variations:

- Use letters of the alphabet.
- Count backwards.

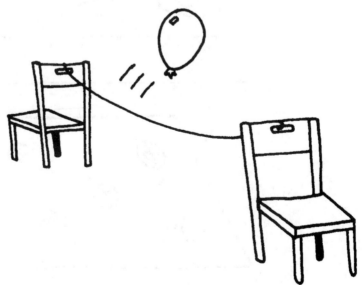

Money Pots

Materials:

- six coins of each—pennies, nickels, dimes, and quarters
- masking tape
- an old towel
- four plastic containers
- measuring tape

Your child is in her counting house sorting out her money.

Directions

Tape a three-foot (1 m) line of masking tape on one side of your living room. Spread the towel on the floor behind the line to protect your carpeting. Mix the coins and put them on the towel. Across the room, place the four plastic containers equal distances apart. Before you begin the game, take time to discuss the differences in the coins—size, color, edges, weight, pictures, and value. As you identify them, tape a different coin to the outside of each plastic container. When you say go, your child grabs a coin and calls out what it is as she drops it into the correct money pot. She then runs back to the pile and grabs another coin. Add some fast-paced music for fun.

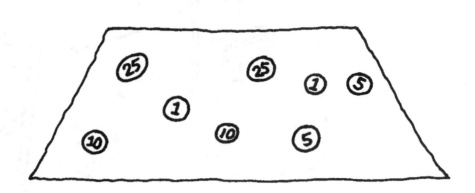

Match Me

Material:

- pairs of objects that begin with the same letter sound—book/ball, pillow/pear
- strands of different colored yarn, each four yards (3.7 m) long
- yardstick
- scissors
- masking tape

The ball is on one side of the room. The book is on the other. Your child identifies and connects their beginning sounds.

Directions

Find five pairs of objects where each pair starts with the same letter sound. Place one object from each pair in a row on the left side of the room. The objects should be one foot (30 cm) apart. Place the other half of the pair in a row on the right side of the room. Be sure that the pairs are not in the same order. Tape one end of the yarn beside the objects on the left. Leave the yarn in a pile next to the object. Have your child identify each object and its beginning letter sound. Do this for both rows. Then, starting in the left row with the ball, tell your child he will be trying to find the object across the room that starts with the same sound as "ball." Emphasize the beginning sound, /b/. When your child identifies the matching sound of "book," he connects the two objects with a line of yarn. Be sure to pull the yarn slightly taut and to tape it beside the matching object. Continue with the next pair of matching sounds.

Beginner's Box

Materials:

- a shoebox
- construction paper
- marker
- scissors
- masking tape

Enjoy a game of seek-and-find around the house as your child identifies beginning sounds.

Directions

Cut eight squares out of the construction paper. On every piece of construction paper write the same letter, such as "b." Place all of these pieces of paper into the shoebox. Then tell your child you have a special box—a box that holds the beginning sound of many objects in your house. Have your child open the box and identify the letter and the sound that it makes. Next, your child hunts for objects around the house that begins with that same sound as the letters in the box (bed, bread, box, broom, and block). Place a piece of masking tape on the paper letter and have your child place the letter on the object. Everywhere in your house can be fair game in the search. Leave the letters up for a while. You may find that your child will play the game on her own. Each day can be a new letter.

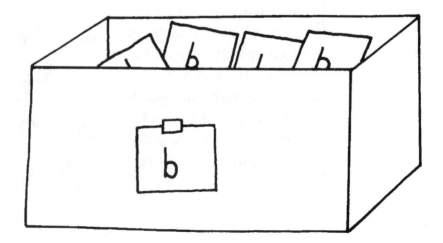

Prepositional Box

Materials:

- cardboard box big enough for your child to sit in (Television boxes work great. Check appliance or rent-to-own stores for empty boxes.)
- masking tape
- utility knife

Your child is in the box, under the box, and crawling right through the box into understanding prepositional phrases.

Directions

Find a large cardboard box. Tape the box closed. On a side that does not have flaps, cut an opening large enough for your child to crawl through but be sure to leave about three inches (8 cm) of cardboard all the way around the edge. This will help keep the box sturdy. Opposite the side with the opening, cut another opening so your child will be able to crawl through the box. Place the box in the middle of the living room. Then start giving your child directions using prepositional phrases (phrases that include directional words). For a list of common prepositions, see the game House of Prepositions on page 121.

Possible Directions:

- Crawl through the box.
- Stand in the box.
- Sit beside the box.
- Place your hand on the box.
- Put your hand under the box.
- Wave your hand above the box.
- Stick your foot below the box.
- Run around the box.
- Slip into the box.
- Lie next to the box.
- Run near the box.
- Get behind the box.
- Squat by the box.
- Walk toward the box.
- Skip away from the box.

Body Language

Materials:

- alphabet flash cards (or index cards and markers if you want to make your own)

He bends and twists and turns. He becomes the letter "T."

Directions

Show your child a card with an uppercase letter written on it. Your child tries to create the letter shape with his body. He may use every part of his body or he may use just a part of his body. For instance, he can make a "Y" standing straight with his arms raised in the air in a "v," or he can make an "O" with just his arms. Encourage him to sit, stand, or lie down to create his letters. Be sure to try a few yourself.

Variations:

- Use flash cards with lowercase letters.

- Use flash cards with shapes.

- You say the sound and your child must try to make the letter.

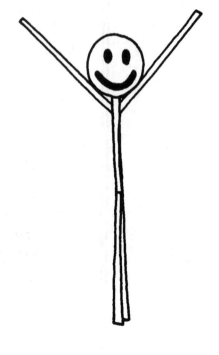

Station Stop

Materials:

• yarn

Follow the yarn road.

Directions

Start by tying the yarn to a door handle. A closet or an outside door is best. You will be creating a road your child will follow. This yarn road will have "station stops" where you will tie off the yarn before going on to the next "station stop." Let's say the first room you enter is the living room. Your first "station stop" is the couch. You pull the yarn slightly taut and wrap it around the leg of the couch. Your next "station stop" is the table. Continue this throughout the house until you decide to end the road. You could end it at the table, where your child will have lunch or maybe the road will end at your child's bed where he will take a nap. Your child starts the road at the door handle. He follows the road to the couch, his first "station stop." He must tell you everything that is associated with the couch. You sit on it; Daddy falls asleep on it; it is soft; more than one person can sit on it at a time; it is purple with orange stripes; it has pillows on it; it has six legs; and dust bunnies live under it. He then follows the road to the next "station stop" and continues this game until he reaches his destination.

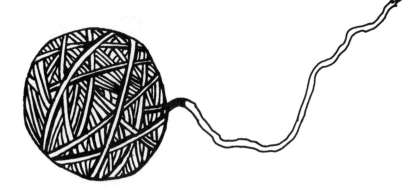

Bop, Hop, Pop

Materials:

- masking tape
- yardstick

Beginning sounds are just a hop and a pop away.

Directions

With the masking tape, make a circle one foot (30 cm) in diameter. Then make three one-foot (30 cm) squares in a row touching the circle and each other. End with another circle one foot (30 cm) in diameter. Start by telling your child a word. Let's say you choose the word "ball." Ask your child what the beginning sound of the word "ball" is. He identifies the sound as /b/. Tell your child that he will be hopping through the shapes and as he hops, he will be saying the word and its beginning sound. In the circles he says the word. In the squares he says the beginning sound. It should sound (and look) like this: "Ball (hops into circle), /b/ (hops into square), /b/ (hops into next square), /b/ (hops into third square), ball (hops into last circle)."

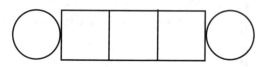

Variation:

- Do ending sounds and have your child hop backward through the shapes.

Mirror, Mirror

Materials:

• a full length mirror

Making faces and sticking out her tongue becomes a learning experience.

Directions

Have your child stand facing the mirror. To begin with, you may want to stand behind her so that she can see you, too. Tell your child to make a face that shows she is happy. You do the same. Tell her to add some body actions that also shows she is happy. She may clap her hands or jump up and down. Have your child create as many different facial and body expressions as she can. This is one game she can do on her own anytime.

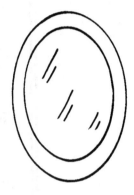

Possible Expressions:

• happy, excited, sad, mad, surprised, scared, nervous, confused, hot, cold, sleepy, tired, angry, annoyed, bored, tasted something yucky, stepped on a hot sidewalk, slipped on the ice, won a prize, lost a game.

Variation:

• Your child does an action and you guess what she is trying to express.

Float, Flutter, Fly

Materials:

- radio or tape player
- scarves or light weight squares of fabric

Following the leader will have your child dancing all over the place.

Directions

Play music with variations in tempo and mood. Music without words works best. Classical or jazz or marches are great. *The Nutcracker* is always a fun selection. Give your child one or two scarves and have her hold them by one of the corners. Turn the music on and begin moving. To begin with, have your child follow your lead and try to copy your movements. Move with the beat of the music. Use your arms and the scarves. If the music repeats a pattern, you do a repetitive movement. If the music speeds up, your movements should speed up. If the music seems sad, your movements should seem sad. Dance on your tiptoes if the melody hits high notes. Drop down to a crouch if the music hits low notes. It is all right to point things out to your child about the music, but be careful not to talk too much. You want her to be listening to the music. After a while, have your child be the leader.

The Farmer Takes an "L"

Materials:

- paper plates
- markers
- masking tape
- measuring tape

The favorite game "The Farmer in the Dell" takes on a new twist to teach your child her letters.

Directions

Create a circle with masking tape that measures six feet (1.5 m) in diameter. Write the uppercase letters of the alphabet on the paper plates and place them around the outside of the circle. Have your child stand in the center of the circle. Sing this little ditty:

> *"The farmer takes an 'L.'*
> *The farmer takes an 'L.'*
> *Hi-Ho! The cheery-o!*
> *The farmer takes an 'L'."*

As you and your child sing the song, your child must run and find the "L," hop on it, and return to the center before you finish the song. Repeat the song using a new letter each time.

Variations:

- Use the lowercase letters of the alphabet.
- Draw shapes on the paper plates.
- Write numbers on the paper plates.
- Use both uppercase and lowercase letters and have your child hop on both letters before the end of the song.

Flight of the Bumblebee

Materials:

- masking tape
- construction paper
- scissors
- measuring tape

Just like the bees in your garden, your child will be buzzing down this path.

Directions

Create a path with the masking tape. It should be 12 feet (3 m) long. Make the path curvy, not straight, with the curves making the path 2½ feet (76 cm) wide. Cut out six construction paper flowers. Tape the flowers to the path every two feet (61 cm). Explain that this is a garden path and that your child is a creature who lives in the garden and is traveling from flower to flower. You call out a creature, such as a bee, and your child buzzes down the path from flower to flower acting like a bee. When he reaches the end of the path, he returns to where he started, and you give him the name of another creature. If your child doesn't know what a certain insect or creature looks like or how it acts, look it up in the encyclopedia or in a book from the library.

Possible Creatures:

- grasshopper, caterpillar, cricket, beetle, firefly, fly, any bird, earthworm, rabbit, spider, butterfly, ladybug, slug, sow bug, centipede, and moth.

Tunnel Time

Materials:

- a cardboard box large enough for your child to crawl through (a television or other large appliance box works great)
- flash cards: uppercase and lowercase letters (or you can make your own using index cards and markers)

Your child grabs a letter, crawls through a tunnel, and finds its match on the other side.

Directions

Fold in the flaps on both ends of the box to create a tunnel. Place the cardboard box in the middle of the room. On the left side of the box, spread out the uppercase flash cards. On the right side of the box, spread out the lowercase flash cards. Have your child start on the side with the uppercase letters. You call out a letter. Your child finds the uppercase letter, grabs the flash card, and crawls through the tunnel. When she reaches the other side, she finds the matching lowercase card and puts them on top of the box. Start over with a new letter.

Variations:

- Use matching sets on the flash cards. Create them on index cards with markers. For example, draw a set of five hearts on one index card and place it to the left of the box. Draw a set of five squares on another index card and put it on the right side of the box.

- Match numerals and the words that spell them out.

- Match numerals and sets that have the same amount.

Animal Crackers

Materials:

- a cardboard box large enough for your child to fit in (a television or other large appliance box works great)

A big box and a lot of animal actions set the stage for lots of fun.

Directions

Fold the flaps in on both ends of the box. Place the box in the middle of the living room. Have your child get into the box. Tell him the box is a box of animal crackers and he will become the animals that are inside the box. Call out an animal name. Your child crawls out of the box and when he emerges, he becomes that animal. Let's say you call out, "elephant." Your child walks and sounds like an elephant as he roams around the room for a few minutes. When he returns to the box, he ceases to be an elephant. Call out another animal name and he transforms into yet another animal.

A Fast Shuffle

Materials:

- 52 paper plates
- markers
- masking tape

Your child's need for speed will be satisfied as she matches uppercase and lowercase letters.

Directions

Using a marker, write each uppercase letter on different paper plates. Make the letters as large as you can. Do the same for the lowercase letters. The letters need not be the same color. Lay the uppercase letters on one side of the floor in the living room. Do the same with the lowercase letters on the other side of the room. Mark the center of the room with a small piece of masking tape and have your child start there. Call out, "On your mark, get set, find the uppercase letter 'B.'" Your child runs and picks up the plate with the uppercase "B" on it. Next, have her find the lowercase "b." She must then quickly hand the matching pair to you and return to the center of the room.

Variations:

- Start with only six pairs of letters.
- Use numerals and sets—a number 3 on one paper plate and three hearts drawn on another.
- Use big shapes and their matching small shapes.

To the Top Hop

Materials:

• stairs

The goal is to get to the top of the stairs. All your child has to do is think of a rhyming word.

Directions

Discuss with your child what it means when you say that one word rhymes with another. You may want to read a few rhyming books or poems first. Your child starts by standing at the bottom of the stairs. Explain that you will tell him a word and he must tell you a word that rhymes with it. For example, you say the word "hat" and your child answers with the word "bat." If he gives you a word that rhymes, he gets to hop up to the next step. If the word does not rhyme, he must try again. Continue all the way to the top of the stairs.

Variations:

• Use antonyms (opposites).

• Use synonyms (words that mean the same such as little and small).

The Race Is On

Materials:

- paper plates
- markers
- alphabet flash cards
- number flash cards

It's just like a board game. Your child lands on a square, picks a card, gives a correct answer, and can move ahead.

Directions

You will need 10 plain white paper plates and 10 paper plates with a big X drawn in the middle of each of them. Lay the paper plates out on the floor alternating them plain, X, plain, X, etc. The plates need to be a stepping distance apart and in a relatively straight or slightly curvy line. Next, shuffle your deck of alphabet flash cards and place them face down on the floor. Then shuffle your number flash cards and place them face down on the floor. If you do not have flash cards, you can make them easily by using unlined index cards. Have your child start by standing on the first paper plate. When your child steps on a plain plate, you take the first card off the top of the number pile and show it to her. She must identify the number correctly. If she does, she hops to the next plate. If she does not, you tell her the correct number, return the card to the bottom of the pile, and choose another one. She must be able to correctly identify the number before she can move on. When she steps on a plate with an X on it, you choose a card from the alphabet pile. This process continues until your child reaches the last plate and wins the race.

On My Trip to Jupiter . . .

Materials:

- paper plates
- markers

A shortened version of this alphabet game is a great challenge for your child.

Directions

As large as you can, write the letters of the alphabet on paper plates using different colored markers. Use one letter for each plate. Choose any three letters and place them in a row on the floor. Discuss the letters and the sounds they make. Discuss words that begin with that sound. Let's say you choose the letters T, Z, and B. Start the game by saying, "On my trip to Jupiter . . ." and as your child hops onto the first letter "T," he must say, "I brought . . ." and he fills in something that begins with that letter. It can be anything—tennis ball, toys, truck, turtle, Tommy, tacos. He then starts over. "On my trip to Jupiter, I brought a turtle (hops on the T), and a zebra (hops on the Z)." Again, he goes back to the beginning and says, "On my trip to Jupiter, I brought a turtle (hops on T), a zebra (hops on Z), and a bike (hops on B)." Choose three new letters and go on another trip.

Variation:

- Use more letters.
- Learn more about Jupiter in the encyclopedia or check out a book from the library.

Group Hoops

Materials:

- masking tape
- measuring tape

Hopping from one hoop to another, your child will be naming items in a group.

Directions

Create five circles in a row. Each circle will measure two feet (61 cm) in diameter. Have your child stand outside the first circle in the row. Tell her you will be picking a category and she must hop into each circle and call out something that belongs in that category or group. For example, you choose the category of animals. Your child hops into the first hoop and calls out, "polar bear." She hops into the next hoop and says, "rabbit." She continues until she has hopped into all five hoops and has named five different animals. She then starts over with a new category.

Possible Categories:

- things with wheels, things that fly, things you eat, things that have an odor, things that are heavy, things you cook, things in a house, things on a car, things at the grocery store, things at the library, friends, relatives, songs, words that begin with a given letter, green things, round things, things you play with, living things, things that jump, wet things, things in the sky, sad things, things Daddy does, places you go, loud things, small things, things you know how to do, and things you want for your birthday.

Pop Out the Top

Materials:

- a cardboard box, large enough for your child to fit in (a television box or large appliance box works great)

Hop. Chop. Crop. Each time your child pops out the top, he learns a new rhyme.

Directions

Fold in the top flaps of the box. Place the box in the middle of the floor with the open end up. Help your child get into the box. Have him crouch down inside the box so that he can't be seen from the outside. Then call out a word, such as "top." Your child must think of a word that rhymes with "top" and then jump up and call out the rhyming word, such as "pop." Before beginning this game, you might want to read a few rhyming books or poems that contain rhyming words.

Variations:

- Have your child pop out the top with the number that comes next. You say "six." He says "seven."

- Have your child pop out the top with the letter that comes next. You say "c." He says "d."

Creature Feature

Materials:

- pictures of creatures (mammals, fish insects, birds, reptiles, amphibians, etc.)
- masking tape
- yardstick

Language development and creative play go hand in hand, as your child becomes the animal she sees.

Directions

Collect pictures of creatures. They can come from your child's magazines and books. They can be postcards, posters, or paintings. They can be in encyclopedias or science books. Books and magazines from the library are a good source. Collect a variety of creatures: insects, birds, fish, reptiles, amphibians, mammals, or spiders. Using the masking tape, make one three-foot (.9 m) square. Two feet (61 cm) away, create a rectangle that is three by ten feet (.9 m x 9.2 m). Tell your child that the square is the "looks like" box and the rectangle is the "acts like" box. Show your child a picture of a creature, such as a butterfly. Your child hops into the square and describes the butterfly. She might say, "It has wings. It is black and orange. It has two antennae and six legs. It is beautiful." Then she hops into the rectangle. She becomes a butterfly as she flutters and floats from one end of the rectangle to the other. Encourage sounds and movement. Discuss how the creature would act in different situations such as landing on a flower, being frightened by a dog, or being chased by a butterfly net. Show your child a new picture and start again.

Tangled Up

Materials:

- balloon shapes cut from different colored construction paper
- yarn to match each color of the balloons
- yardstick
- masking tape
- scissors

Through a maze of colored strings, your child will find his way to recognizing different colors.

Directions

Cut a large balloon shape from each color of construction paper. Cut strands of yarn six yards (5.5 m) in length. Tape the matching color of yarn to the backside of each balloon. Tape the red balloon at the edge of the room. Create a trail of red yarn throughout the room using several twists and turns. Do this with each balloon and its matching string. The different colored yarns may overlap each other. Do one color at a time to prevent the strings from getting too tangled. Try to have all of the strings end up in the same area. The balloons may be anywhere in the room. Start by having your child identify the color of each balloon. Then pick a yarn color, say red. He identifies the balloon that is attached to the red string and follows the red yarn path through the tangle of other stings to find the red balloon. As he walks along the path, have your child say, "I'm looking for my red balloon," over and over until he finds the red balloon.

Variation:

- Add more colors—pink, purple, black, brown, gray, white, etc.

Shape Box

Materials:

- a cardboard box, large enough for your child to fit in (a television box works great)
- utility knife
- masking tape
- markers
- felt
- scissors
- ruler

Matching shapes with a little twist will keep your child interested in the fun of learning.

Directions

Tape the box shut. Using the markers, draw a large shape on each side of the box, except the taped side, which will be the bottom. Make the shapes eight inches (20 cm). The shapes should include a square, rectangle, triangle, circle, and an oval. Next, cut along the outline of the shape to create a door. For example, you will cut along three sides of the square but not the fourth side. That side will act as the hinges for the square door. Make a door handle tab with masking tape so your child can open and close the doors. Do this for all the shapes. Then cut out shapes from the felt. Use the same shapes as the ones on the doors. Make six of each shape. Next, place the shape box in the middle of the room. Spread the felt shapes randomly over the floor. Tell your child to find a square and put it into the square door. She chooses any square, opens the square door and drops in the felt shape. Continue until all of the felt shapes are in the box.

Variations:

- Remove the tape from the box so your child can go inside the box and push the shapes out through the doors. She may need a flashlight to find the shapes.
- Add more shapes such as hearts, stars, and diamonds.

Blanket Board

Materials:

- a blanket with a fuzzy nap
- a door
- different colored felt
- scissors
- ruler

A blanket becomes a giant felt board, and your child's imagination grows.

Directions

Cut different shapes from the colored felt. Make a variety of each color. Include at least two sizes of circles, squares, triangles, and rectangles from each color. Make the large shapes at least three inches (8 cm) and your smaller shapes no less than one and a half inches (3.84 cm). Your child will be using these shapes to create pictures such as ice cream cones, houses, animals, and snowmen, so keep that in mind when creating the different shapes. Next, toss a blanket over the top of an open door. Anchor the blanket by closing the door just enough to hold the blanket in place or by using masking tape. Be sure the blanket has a fuzzy nap so that the felt pieces stay in place. Give your child the shapes and let him explore. Then have him sort the shapes by color, by size, and then by shape.

Variations:

- Create patterns.
- Have your child make up stories and create pictures using the shapes.
- Create addition and subtraction problems using the shapes.

Shape Up

Materials:

- construction paper
- scissors
- masking tape
- shoebox

Things in your house will shape up as your child sees your doors as rectangles.

Directions

Cut different shapes out of construction paper (ten squares, ten rectangles, eight circles, and four triangles). Place the different shapes into the shoebox. Tell your child you have a special box. The box holds the shapes of many objects in your house. Have your child open the box, choose a shape, and identify what it is. Have her describe the shape's characteristics. How many corners does it have? How many sides does it have? How many angles does it have? Then have your child go on a hunt throughout the house to find objects that match the shape she chose from the box. When she finds an object that matches, she must tape the paper shape to the object. Choose another shape from the box and start again. You may choose to start by having all of one shape in the shoebox.

Variation:

- Use colored construction paper and hunt for colors.

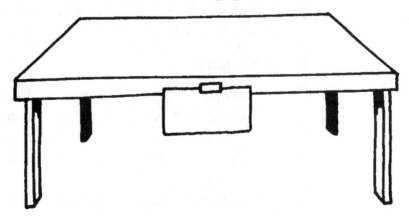

Behind Door #1 . . .

Materials:

- different colored construction paper
- white paper
- scissors
- masking tape
- lower kitchen cupboard doors
- ruler

If you don't mind a few doors slamming, your child will have a great time matching.

Directions

Cut five pairs of different shapes from the construction paper. Make them at least five inches (13 cm) long. Make each pair of shapes a different color. Possible shapes may include squares, circles, rectangles, triangles, or ovals. From the white paper, cut five four-inch (10 cm) squares. Write one number on each white square starting with 1 and ending with 5. Tape these numbered papers on the outside of your lower kitchen cupboard doors. On the inside of those numbered doors, place one shape from each pair of shapes. Place the other five shapes in the middle of the kitchen floor. Have your child stand near the shapes. Call out, "Behind door number 1 . . . " Your child runs to door #1, opens it, and grabs the colored shape. He must then find its match among the shapes on the floor. Continue calling out the numbers until all of the shapes have been found. Mix them up and start again.

Safety Note: *Be sure there is nothing breakable or potentially harmful that can fall out when the cupboard door is opened.*

Variations:

- Make a memory game of it. First, have your child check behind all the doors. Then show him a shape. Tell him to see it he can find the shape behind one of the doors. He checks until he finds the matching shape.
- Add more shapes if you have more doors.

Color Patrol

Materials:

- different colored shirts or hats or gloves
- construction paper
- white paper
- scissors
- masking tape
- box of crayons
- clothespins

The color for the day is chosen, and everywhere your child looks he finds it.

Directions

Choose a color for the day. Let's say it is blue. Cut six circles from the blue construction paper and tape them to the clothespins. Also, cut a piece in the shape of a badge. Tape the badge to your child's shirt and tell him he is now on "color patrol" for the color blue. If you have a blue hat or blue gloves or a blue shirt, have him wear them. Next, discuss the fact that there are different shades of blue. Demonstrate this by showing your child all the different shades of blue from his box of crayons. Have him scribble on some white paper so he can see the differences. Then clip the clothespins to his shirt and send him on patrol to look for blue things around the house. Whenever he finds something that is blue, he clips a clothespin to it, and then off he goes to find another. To really emphasize the color of the day, wear blue clothes, drink blue drinks, and eat as much blue food as you can. Tomorrow, choose another color.

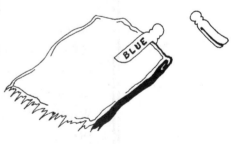

Memory

Materials:

- different colored construction paper
- scissors
- masking tape
- yardstick

She will be hopping all the way to remembering her colors.

Directions

Create a row of five connected squares with the masking tape. Make them one-foot (30-cm) squares. Cut three more squares out of each color of construction paper. Make them three inches (8 cm) on each side. Have your child stand at one end of the row of squares. You choose any color square of construction paper and lay it in the square. Your child then hops into the first square of the masking tape row and calls out the color. Let's say the colored square is blue. She then returns to where she started. You lay down another colored square, this time yellow. Your child hops into the first square and calls out "blue"; then she hops into the second square and calls out "yellow." She returns to her starting position at the beginning of the row and you start the process all over again. Continue until there is a color assigned to all five squares. You may repeat colors. Then have your child return to her starting position, but this time you remove the first colored square. Your child must remember the color that was assigned to the first square in the row without the construction paper reminder. Repeat this process until your child can hop through the five squares without any construction paper reminders.

Special Delivery

Materials:

- lunch bags
- different colored construction paper
- scissors
- masking tape
- ice cream bucket or pail with a handle

Delivering the mail will take on a shape of its own.

Directions

Draw a different shape on each of the paper bags. The shapes may include a square, rectangle, triangle, circle, diamond, heart, oval, and star. Cut at least six of each shape from the construction paper. Each shape should be different colors and different sizes. Next, tape the bags to the doors in your house. If you don't have enough doors, backs of chairs or edges of tables will do. Be sure to mix the shapes up, then have your child deliver them to their correct mailbox bags.

Variations:

- Once your child has delivered all the shapes, have her sort each bag of shapes by color and then by size.

- Create patterns by putting the shapes in a repeating order.

Musical Shapes

Materials:

- paper plates
- masking tape
- markers
- radio or tape/CD player
- measuring tape

The music begins. Your child skips. He dances. He jogs. But when the music stops, your child must find his shape.

Directions

Using the masking tape, create a circle on the floor that is six feet (5.5 m) in diameter. On the paper plates, make different colored shapes. Possible shapes may include a square, rectangle, circle, triangle, heart, oval, star, and diamond. Tape the plates to the floor around the outside of the circle. Start the music. Your child walks, jogs, skips, or dances around the inside of the circle until the music stops. Then you call out a shape and your child must run to the correct shape. Start the music and begin again.

Variations:

- Use colors.
- Use the letters of the alphabet.
- Use numbers or sets.

Paper Hearts

Materials:

- different colored construction paper
- scissors

Big hearts, little hearts, red hearts, blue hearts, and your child learns from them all.

Directions

Cut six small, six medium, and six large hearts from each color of construction paper. Mix them all together and have your child sort the hearts into groups according to different attributes. Start with color and then try size. Next, start a pattern with the hearts. Start with a two-colored pattern of the same size such as large red heart, large blue heart, large red heart, large blue heart. Then start at the left and say the pattern together. When you get to the end, ask your child what comes next. She will say that the large red heart comes next. Start at the left and say the pattern together. Again, ask her what comes next. She will say that a large blue heart comes next. Repeat the pattern one more time and then try another pattern. Slowly introduce size and more colors into your patterns.

Variations:

- Use the paper hearts for counting.
- Use the paper hearts to identify colors.
- Use the paper hearts to create sets.
- Use the paper hearts to add and subtract.

Disappearing Act

Materials:

- household objects
- stuffed animals or toys
- large cardboard box

Your child's favorite toys are put into a pile. He leaves the room and returns to find one missing. Which one is it?

Directions

Gather eight familiar objects from around the house. You can use toys, clothes, books, stuffed animals, or even silverware. Lay them out on the living room floor. Have your child study them. Have him describe the objects by their name, color, shape, or any other noticeable feature. Then tell your child to leave the room. He can run to his bedroom and back. While he is gone, place one of the objects from the group into the cardboard box. When your child returns, have him identify the object that disappeared into the box.

Variations:

- Use more objects.
- Move the objects around after your child studies them.

Taped Tightrope

Materials:

- masking tape

Your child will put on a balancing act as she moves from room to room on her tightrope.

Directions

Create a continuous path throughout your house by placing masking tape on the floor. A great place to start is your child's bedroom right next to her bed. Make the path straight, curvy, crooked, and broken. Let the path lead to the bathroom, her chair, and the backdoor. You can have her start anywhere on the tightrope. Explain and demonstrate how you walk along a tightrope (pointing toes with each step and arms straight out to the side at shoulder height). Have her walk the tightrope all around the house. Leave the path in place for a while. She'll jump out of bed to start on the right path for the day.

Variations:

- Skip, hop, run, gallop, walk backwards, tiptoe, make giant steps, or walk sideways along the tightrope.

- Do step patterns along the path: tiptoe, tiptoe, giant step, tiptoe, tiptoe, giant step . . .

Button Up

Materials:

- old clothes with buttons, zippers, and ties
- timer

A day of dress-up and your child takes a step toward independence.

Directions

Collect old clothes, preferably adult clothes. Look for shirts or jackets with big buttons or zippers. Gather belts that tie and buckle and shoes that tie. Collect anything that will give your child the practice he needs to get dressed. Put all of the clothes into a pile on the floor. Tell him that he is going to be racing against the clock. Set your timer for five minutes (more or less depending upon your child's abilities). Your child's goal will be to put on as many clothes as he can before the timer goes off. If your child has a little trouble, you may give him some assistance. Perhaps you can start a button through a hole, and then your child finishes it. You may choose to practice a skill before you set the timer.

Variations:

- Set the timer for three minutes and have your child put on only a certain type of clothing. He must search through the pile for, let's say, something with a zipper and put it on before the timer goes off.

All Four on the Floor

Materials:

• masking tape

A creative crawl will get your child across your living room floor.

Directions

Place a strip of tape on the right side of the room. Place another strip, parallel to the first strip, on the left side of the room. Have your child stand behind the line on the right side and tell him to walk across the room. Ask, "How many parts of your body were touching the floor as you walked across the room?" His answer should be two. Challenge him to get across the room with only one part of his body touching the floor. He might try hopping on one foot. Encourage him to be creative. Have him try different ways of crossing the floor with up to six parts of his body touching the floor. He may even figure out how to cross the room having 20 parts of his body touching the floor (On tiptoes and fingertips, of course!).

Mommy's Mirror

Materials:

• none

Your child becomes the splitting image of you.

Directions

Stand so that you and your child are facing each other. Explain to your child that he is the mirror and that you are looking into the mirror. His job is to copy everything that you do. Start easily and slowly. Make your actions slow motion. Put your finger on your nose, your hand on your head, or pretend you are wiping a window. Whatever your actions, your mirror image (your child) must copy what you do. Include facial features, but no voices. Next, switch roles and you become the mirror and your child initiates the actions.

Just One More

Materials:

• none

Your child does one action, two actions, and then just one more.

Directions

You will be the leader. You start out with an action that your child must repeat. Let's say you hop forward. Your child hops forward. Then you start over with the same action and add another. You hop forward and then you hop backwards. Your child hops forward and then backwards. You repeat the first two actions and add a third. You hop forward, backwards, and then you squat down. Your child does the same. You continue starting with your first action and adding another until your child misses an action. Start again with your child being the leader.

Box Hop

Materials:

- masking tape
- measuring tape

Learning left and right and front and back is just a jump away.

Directions

With the masking tape, create two rectangles that intersect to make what looks like a plus sign. The rectangles should be 45 inches (120 cm) long and 15 inches (40 cm) wide. Their intersection will create a 15-inch (40-cm) square in the middle. Have your child stand in the center square. Then start giving him directions that include front, back, left, and right. After each direction, your child will return to the center square. For example, tell your child to jump to the front, then to the center. From there tell him to jump left and then center. Start out slowly and then speed up.

```
              ┌────────┐
              │        │
              │ front  │
              │        │
    ┌─────────┼────────┼─────────┐
    │         │        │         │
    │  left   │ center │  right  │
    │         │        │         │
    └─────────┼────────┼─────────┘
              │        │
              │  back  │
              │        │
              └────────┘
```

Variations:

- Change how he jumps: big jump, little jump, high jump, low jump, loud jump, or soft jump. Continue to include the directions of front, back, left, right, and center.

The Missing Egg

Materials:

- different colored plastic eggs

Which one is the missing egg?

Directions

Place one egg of each color in a pile on the floor. Have your child study the pile of eggs. Talk about the colors. Tell her she is going to have to use her memory for this game. Have your child leave the room. Remove one egg from the pile without moving any of the other eggs and hide it out of sight. Call your child back into the room. Ask her what color egg is missing from the pile. When she identifies it, return the egg to the pile, mix it up, and have her study the pile again. Send her to the other room to play again.

Variations:

- You leave the room and your child hides the egg.

- After your child leaves the room, remove the egg, and then mix up the pile of eggs.

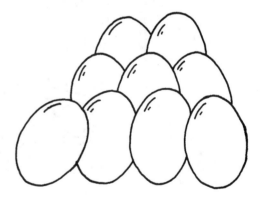

Magazine I Spy

Materials:

- magazines with interesting, detailed pictures

Here is a little quieter game that will increase your child's observation of details.

Directions

Gather together several magazines that have pictures with lots of details and color. Your local library probably has some great kids' magazines that can be checked out. Find a spot where you and your child can sit or lie close together. Start out by discussing the details of the picture. Point out things that your child might not observe. Discuss the shape of things, the color, the shadowing, the texture, and funny or interesting details. Then on the same picture, play a game of I Spy. Say, "I spy something..." then choose a color or a shape. You can even spy the uses of things such as, "I spy something that you can eat." Then your child must start listing the objects in the picture that answer your clue. When your child guesses your spy, it is his turn to spy something.

Hands Up

Materials:

• none

A fast paced game has your child following all kinds of directions.

Directions

Have your child stand. Explain that you will be giving her a series of directions about what to do with her hands and that she must follow these directions as quickly as she can. For example, you say, "Hands up," and your child raises her hands over her head. You say, "Hands down," and she drops her hands to her sides. Start out slowly with the directions and then speed up. Have fun and be creative.

Possible Directions:

• hands down, hands forward, hands down at your sides, hands on your shoulders, hands on your knees, hands in front, hands in back, hands on the floor, hands on your hips, hands on your head, hands over your ears, hands beneath your feet, hands together, hands on the side of your head, hands on your thighs, hands between your knees, and hand on your tummy.

1, 2, 3, Follow Me

Materials:

- masking tape
- yardstick

Ready, set, go! Follow three directions in a row.

Directions

Starting at one end of the room, make five masking tape shapes measuring two feet (61 cm). Possible shapes may include a square, circle, triangle, rectangle, oval, heart, diamond, or star. Tell your child he will be starting at one end of the shape row and that he must make it through all five of the shapes and reach the other side. To do this, he must be able to follow three directions in a row. Your child starts by standing in the square (the first shape). Let's say you give him these three directions: Put your hands on your head, shut your eyes, and hop once. Your child must wait until you have given him all three directions before doing them. If he gets them all right, he advances to the next shape on the floor where you give him three new directions to follow.

Variations:

- Reverse roles and have your child give you the directions.

- If your child is having problems with following three directions, start with two.

Hokey Left and Pokey Right

Materials:

- red sock
- blue sock
- red balloon
- blue balloon

Your child will Hokey Pokey her way to knowing left and right.

Directions

Hunt down a red sock and a blue sock. Be sure to find some socks for yourself! Any old sock will do, even Dad's. Blow up a red balloon and a blue balloon. Have your child put the red sock on her right foot and the blue sock on her left foot. Then have her hold the red balloon in her right hand and the blue balloon in her left hand. Start doing the Hokey Pokey together. Tell your child she will be starting with her right hand which is holding a red balloon. Every time the song tells her to move her right hand, she will be moving her red balloon. Sing the following song:

> *"You put your right hand in. You put your right hand out.*
> *You put your right hand in, and you shake it all about.*
> *You do the Hokey Pokey, and you turn yourself around.*
> *That's what it's all about."*

Continue with the blue balloon and the left hand. Then include the feet with the colored socks.

Need music? Try *Wee Sing and Play* by Pamela Conn Beall and Susan Hagen Nipp, published in 1981 by Price Stern Sloan of Los Angeles.

Five Sense Shoebox

Materials:

- a shoebox
- familiar objects
- towel or scarf
- masking tape

Your child will touch, taste, smell, hear, and finally see her way to identifying objects.

Directions

Find a shoebox with a lid. Then collect different household objects that will fit inside the shoebox such as a fork, a glove, a stuffed animal, a banana, or a toothbrush. Do not let your child see any of the objects you have collected. You will also need a towel or scarf to use as a blindfold. Put one of the objects into the shoebox. Let's say you chose the fork. Tape the lid of the shoebox shut. Tell your child that inside the shoebox is something that she could recognize if she could see it, but in this game she must figure out what it is by using her four other senses—hearing, tasting, touching, and smelling. Begin the game by having your child shake the box. What sound does the object make when it hits the walls of the box? Is the object heavy or light? Tie on the blindfold, open the box, and let your child feel the object. Have her describe the object. Is it smooth? It is cold? Have your child smell the object. What kind of odor does it have, if any? Let her taste the object (be sure to wash the object first). Finally, have your child guess the identity of the object. Remove the blindfold and let her find out things about the object she couldn't identify without sight, such as its color.

Body Patterns

Materials:

• none

Stomp, clap, clap. Stomp, clap, clap. Stomp, clap, clap. And the pattern goes on.

Directions

Start simple. Let's say you start with the stomp of a foot and a clap. Have your child repeat the stomp and a clap. Then you do the pattern again. Repeat it a second time: stomp, clap, stomp, clap. Have your child repeat it back to you. Then add to the pattern—stomp, clap, stomp, clap, stomp, clap, stomp—and ask your child what comes next. He should say that a clap comes next. Repeat the pattern together for a while. Then try adding something new to the pattern such as a second clap. Repeat the procedure. Make the patterns fun and interesting.

Patterns to Try:

• hop forward, hop backwards, squat

• clap, turn around, slap knees

• sway left, sway right, jump up in the air

• touch the floor, touch your hips, touch your head

Variation:

• Use just clapping rhythms.

Outdoor Games

Outdoor Games (cont.)

Falling Leaves

Materials:

- fall leaves
- large bucket

An armload of leaves tossed high into the sky leads to a fantastic fall day of counting.

Directions

Rake a few leaves together into a pile. Place a large bucket on the ground. Have your child grab a handful of leaves and toss them high into the air over the bucket. Count only the leaves that fall into the bucket. Dump the bucket and start again.

Variations:

- Use two buckets and decide which bucket has more and which bucket has less.

- Place two buckets on the ground. Add the leaves in the two buckets together.

Easy Catch

Materials:

- two gallon-sized (4 L) plastic milk or water jug
- a tennis ball
- scissors or utility knife

He catches and counts in this fun game.

Directions

Holding the jug upside down by the handle, create a scoop by cutting the jug as show in the diagram. Do this to both of the jugs. Start the game by standing five feet (1.5 m) away from each other. Toss the ball to your child. He must try to catch the ball in the plastic scoop. When he does, he counts and says, "one." He then tosses it to you. You catch it and say "two," and then toss it back to him. He catches it and counts "three." Continue until one of you misses.

Variations:

- Count by 2's, 5's, or 10's.

- Count backwards.

- As an indoor game, use a foam ball or a rolled-up sock.

Bounce Once, Bounce Twice

Materials:

• a ball

Your child will be bouncing balls and counting bounces.

Directions

Find a flat area outside. Your driveway is always a good place. Begin by having your child watch as you bounce the ball. Count together the number of bounces the ball makes. Start with one bounce and continue through ten. Next, have your child turn around. Tell her to listen as you bounce the ball. Have her count the number of times she hears the ball bounce. Choose numbers randomly from one to ten.

Variation:

• Have your child do her own bouncing and counting.

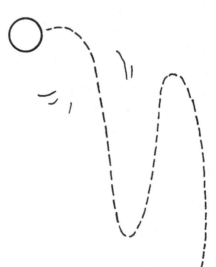

Hippity-Hop Hopscotch

Materials:

- chalk (Note: If you would like to make your own chalk for this game and many others in this section, refer to the recipe on page 153)

Using a slight variation on traditional hopscotch, your child will hop his way to learning his numbers.

Directions

Create a hopscotch formation starting with a square and then centering a horizontal rectangle above the square. DO NOT divide the rectangle into two squares. In the first square, write the number 1. In the rectangle, write the number 2. In the next square, write the number 3, and so on. Each square and each rectangle will have one number written in it. Your child starts by hopping into the square with one foot and calling out the number written in the square. Then he hops into the rectangle, lands on both feet, and calls out the number written in the rectangle. The number of squares and rectangles in your hopscotch depends on how high your child can count. Add a new number every day!

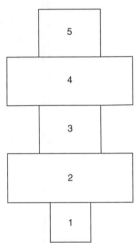

Variations:

- Use the letters of the alphabet—uppercase and lowercase.

- Use colors or shapes.

- Count by 2's, 5's, or 10's.

- Use the sound of the letters

- Count backwards.

Going Fishing

Materials:

- chalk
- measuring tape

A pond of fish will help your child with number recognition.

Directions

Draw the outline of a fishpond 12 feet (3 m) in diameter. Fill it with ten fish. Randomly number the fish 1 though 10. Have your child go fishing for each number. Start with your child standing outside the pond. When you call out a number, your child "swims" over, and jumps on it.

Variations:

- Use stripes or dots instead of numbers.

- In addition to the numbers, make each fish a different color, and have your child "fish" for colors, too.

- Draw one fish swimming in the opposite direction. Have your child identify the "different" fish.

- Draw a unique feature on each fish (smile, frown, hat, crown, tie, huge tail, teeth, glasses, feet, necklaces, etc.). Have your child "fish" for that special feature.

Playing Footsy

Materials:

- chalk
- feet

Learning units of measure start with your child's feet.

Directions

Draw lines of different lengths. Have your child measure the lines by using the length of his foot as the unit of measure. Have your child place his right foot at the beginning of the line and count "one." Then have him place his left heel at the toe of his right foot and count "two." Continue counting with each step until he has measured the entire line.

Variations:

- Measure curved lines.
- Measure the sides of shapes.
- Compare the lengths of the lines.

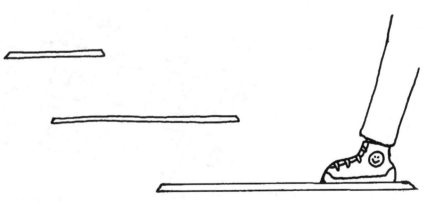

One More, Please

Materials:

- chalk
- yardstick

What comes next in the sequence of numbers?

Directions

Randomly draw eleven 12-inch (30 cm) squares over a chosen area. In each square, randomly write the numbers 0 through 10. Call out a number. When your child is standing on the number, ask her, "What is one more than . . .?" If your child is standing on the number 5, she would answer, "One more than five is six." Repeat until all of the numbers have been called.

Variations:

- When your child is standing on a number, ask her what is one less than that number.

- Ask your child what is two more than the number.

- Ask your child what number comes before the number.

- Ask your child what number comes after the number.

Same or Different

Materials:

- chalk
- yardstick

Your child will easily see the difference in these big sets.

Directions

Create a row with eight pairs of circles. Make each circle 18 inches (46 cm) in diameter. Draw each pair of circles ten inches (25 cm) from the next pair. The circles in the pair itself should be six inches (15 cm) apart. Each circle will contain a set of objects. For example, in the left circle draw five pink hearts. In the right circle draw four pink hearts. Your child will decide if the sets are the same or different. In this case he would tell you that the sets are different. If both circles contained seven carrots each, he would state that the sets are the same. Be sure to ask him why. Then go on to the next pair of circles to find out if their sets are the same or different.

More or Less

Materials:

- chalk
- a five-inch (13 cm) square board
- paint
- paint brush
- yardstick

Which set has more? Which set has less? Your child will easily make the connection.

Directions

This activity uses the same set up as the game, "Same or Different," on page 91. In addition to the row of eight pairs of circles, a five-inch (13 cm) square board painted with the symbol for greater than (>) and less than (<) is needed. As your child analyzes each pair of sets, she must determine if the set on the left has more or less objects than the set on the right. She then places the board with the symbol in the correct position. For example, if the set on the left has three apples and the set on the right has two apples, your child would place the board in the position that states that the left set has more than the right set. Always "read" the sets from left to right. An easy way to remember which way the symbol goes is that the little or pointed end is on the side of the smaller set and the big or open end is on the side of the larger set.

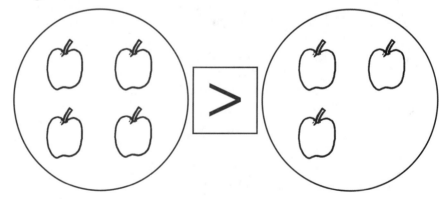

Equal or Not Equal

Materials:

- chalk
- a five-inch (3 cm) square board
- paint
- paint brush

Yes, they're equal; no, they're not. The choice is your child's.

Directions

This activity uses the same set up as the game, "Same or Different," on page 91. In addition to the row of eight pairs of circles, a five-inch (13 cm) square board is needed. On one side of the board, paint an equal sign (=) and on the other side, a not equal sign (an = with a / through it). As your child analyzes each pair of sets, he must determine if the sets are equal or not equal. He then places the board with the correct symbol between the two sets. Be sure to ask what makes the sets equal or not equal.

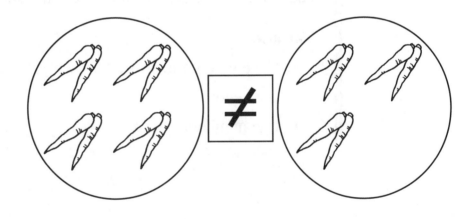

Pencil Patterns

Materials:

- chalk
- yardstick

Challenge your child to predict what comes next in the sequence.

Directions

Draw a three-foot (91 cm) long pencil. Starting at the lead point, draw a long curvy "pencil" line. At the beginning of the line, start a pattern such as red X, blue O, red X, blue O. Start at the beginning of the pattern and "read" it together with your child. After establishing the pattern, ask your child what comes next. He will say, "red X." Read the pattern from the beginning before your child adds the next object in the sequence. Once he has mastered the pattern, stop and start again with a new pattern, a foot (30 cm) down the line. Be sure to challenge your child. Don't make the patterns too easy.

Variations:

- Have your child create his own pattern.
- Use letters.
- Use numbers.
- Use shapes.

Hickory Dickory

Materials:

- chalk
- yardstick

An old rhyme helps your child tell time.

Directions

Draw 12 clock faces in a row. Make the circles 18 inches (46 cm) in diameter. Randomly draw the hands of the clocks showing a different hour on each, ranging from 1 o'clock to 12 o'clock. Sing the "Hickory Dickory Dock" nursery rhyme:

> *"Hickory Dickory Dock.*
> *The mouse ran up the clock.*
> *The clock struck _____ and down he ran.*
> *Hickory Dickory Dock."*

In the blank, fill in the time of the clock that you want your child to run to. It won't always rhyme, but it'll still be fun!

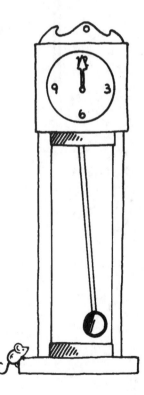

Variations:

- Use the half hours or quarter hours.

Puddle Pond

Materials:

- chalk
- measuring tape

Your child will be fishing for the correct number in this pond.

Directions

Draw a large oval pond measuring approximately five by seven feet (1.5m x 2 m). Draw animals, insects, and other things found in or on the edge of a pond. Your child will be counting the different things so be sure to have a varied number of each (ten bugs, three frogs, eight rocks, etc.). Have your child start on the edge of the pond. Ask him, "How many frogs are in our pond?" He then hops on each frog as he counts them. Do this for each thing in the pond.

Other Things Found in a Pond:

- lilly pads, tadpoles, frogs, logs, turtles, sailboats, rocks, water bugs, fish, ducks, cattails, butterflies

Number Line Hip-Hop

Materials:

- chalk
- measuring tape

Understanding the number line is easy when your child hops through her numbers.

Directions

Create a number line 25 feet (7.7 m) long. Draw a dot at one end and label it zero. Continue making dots at 10-inch (25-cm) intervals, labeling them to 30. (Note: Place an arrow on the end of the number line and tell your child that the numbers on the number line keep getting bigger and don't stop.) Have your child start at "0." Call out a number. Let's say the number is seven. Your child hops to the seven, counting all the way. Ask her what number comes before seven. She then hops back one dot and calls out, "six." Have her return to her original number. Ask her what number comes after seven. She hops forward one dot and calls out, "eight." Have her return to zero and start again.

0 1 2 3 4 5 6 7 8 9 10 11 12 13 14 15 16 17 18 19 20 21 22 23 24 25 26 27 28 29 30

Variations:

- Have your child hop each number, counting as she goes.
- Have your child count backwards (begin at five, then ten, etc.).

Number Line Addition

Materials:

- chalk
- measuring tape

Adding on a number line is as easy as a hop, skip, and a jump.

Directions

Create a number line 25 feet (7.7 m) long. Draw a dot at one end and label it zero. Continue making dots at 10-inch (25-cm) intervals, labeling them to 30. (Note: Place an arrow on the end of the number line and tell your child that the numbers on the number line get bigger and don't stop.) Have your child start at "0." Call out a number such as five. Your child hops on the dots and counts his way to five. Say, "Let's add three more to five." Your child hops and counts three more dots. Ask him what number he landed on, then prompt him to figure out the math equation by saying, "We started with . . . five, we added . . . three more, and now we have . . . eight. Five plus three equals eight." Start over at zero.

```
●┼┼┼┼┼┼┼┼┼┼┼┼┼┼┼┼┼┼┼┼┼┼┼┼┼┼┼┼┼┼→
 0 1 2 3 4 5 6 7 8 9 10 11 12 13 14 15 16 17 18 19 20 21 22 23 24 25 26 27 28 29 30
```

Variation:

- Do the same for subtraction equations.

Mighty Measures

Materials:

- chalk
- yardstick

Measuring becomes a cinch as your child learns to identify an inch.

Directions

You will need a yardstick (meter stick) numbered with inches (cm). Using the yardstick (meter stick), draw lines of different lengths. Make sure the line measures a whole number and not a fraction. Have your child use the yardstick (meter stick) to measure the length of each line. Count the length aloud.

Variations:

- Measure the sides of shapes.
- Use a ruler and measure lines in whole foot increments.
- Measure by the yard (meter).
- You may want to practice with a ruler and lines shorter than 12 inches, if your child doesn't know how to count that high yet.

How Does Your Garden Grow?

Materials:

- chalk
- yardstick

Measuring the height of flowers becomes fun in your child's own sidewalk garden.

Directions

Draw a straight horizontal line eight feet (2.4 m) long. This is the ground. Draw straight vertical stems of different lengths rising up from (and perpendicular to) the "chalk" ground. Be sure that they measure in whole inches (cm) and not fractions. Put a flower on the top of each stem. Add some leaves. Using a yardstick, have your child measure the height of the flower in inches (cm) from the ground up. Have her measure the length of different parts of the flower.

Variation:

- Add "friends" to the garden, such as a butterfly, ant, caterpillar, fly, ladybug, beetle, snake, bird, earthworm, and have your child measure them.

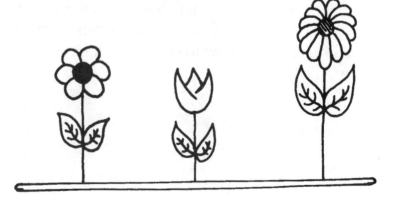

Parts of a Pie

Materials:

- chalk

An introduction to fractions is the beginning to understanding parts and wholes.

Directions

Tell your child this story: Mommy decided to bake a pie for dessert. She baked a strawberry pie (draw a circle with the chalk and color it). After dinner, everyone was so full that nobody ate a piece of the pie. How much pie was left? (All of it; the whole pie; there was one whole pie left—write a number 1 under the pie.). Later that night, you got really hungry. You cut the pie into two big pieces and ate one of the pieces (draw another circle, divide it into two and color one half of the pie). Into how many pieces did you cut the pie? (Two—write a number 2 under the pie as the denominator). How many pieces of pie were left? (One—write a number 1 as the numerator above the number 2. Place a line under the number 1 but above the number 2—write the number as a fraction—$^{1}/_{2}$). Half the pie was left over. One half of the pie was left. One piece out of two was left.

Variations:

- Divide the pie into thirds having $^{1}/_{3}$ or $^{2}/_{3}$ leftover.
- Divide the pie into fourths, having $^{1}/_{4}$, $^{2}/_{4}$, or $^{3}/_{4}$ leftover.

Pedal Patterns

Materials:

- chalk
- a tricycle or riding toy

A stop sign puts a halt to your child's pedaling. But when he identifies the next object in the sequence, he gets to "keep on truckin'."

Directions

Create a road as directed in Truckin' Trikes on page 148. Draw stop signs every 20 feet (5m). When your child comes to a stop sign, he must stop. In order to continue his ride, he must tell you what comes next in the "pattern" that you have created in the road in front of the stop sign. For example, your child rides along, stops, and sees this sequence in the road: O X O X O. He must tell you what comes next. When he gives you the correct answer (X), he may continue until he comes to the next stop sign. Be sure to say the pattern with your child each time he stops. Start with simple patterns, and then increase the difficulty of the pattern.

Variations:

- Use colors as part of the pattern (red X, red O, blue X, blue O, etc.).

- Use shapes (square, circle, triangle, square, circle, triangle, etc.).

- Use different sizes (big square, small square, big square, small square, etc.).

- big square, etc.).

- Use what comes next in the alphabet (a, b, c, etc.) or in counting (1, 2, 3, etc.).

Here's One, Find the Other

Materials:

- nature objects, such as rocks, sticks, maple leaves, dandelions, pine cones, feathers, blades of grass, sand, or flowers.

Your child will enjoy finding pairs in nature.

Directions

Find five objects found outside. Lay the objects out on a picnic table or your steps. Have your child identify each object. If you choose several leaves, be sure your child can see and identify the differences. Then tell your child that she needs to find an object that matches the one on the table. Let's say you start with the dandelion. Your child then searches your yard for a matching dandelion, brings it back, and lays it next to its match.

Knock Down, Take-Away

Materials:

- five empty two-liter plastic soft drink bottles
- ball
- chalk

It's bowling with a difference.

Directions

On a flat surface draw two chalk lines 10 feet (3 m) apart. Behind one of the chalk lines, have your child set up the five plastic soft drink bottles. They may be in any arrangement. Your child stands behind the other chalk line with the ball. Say, "You are starting with five bottles." Then let your child roll the ball toward the bottles. Let's say the ball knocked down three bottles. Say, "You knocked down three bottles." Then ask, "How many are left standing?" Your child should answer, "two." Next say, "That's right, five take away three is two." At the same time, use your fingers to show what happened with the bowling pins. Have your child set up the pins and start again.

Variations:

- Use a different number of pins.
- This game can be played indoors, too.

Two Points

Materials:

- a soft foam ball
- a 12 inch by 12 inch box (30 cm x 30 cm)
- chalk
- measuring tape

He shoots! He scores two points! This is a great way to add up the score.

Directions

Draw a two-foot (61-cm) chalk line on the driveway. Place the box four feet (30 cm) away from the line. Have your child stand behind the line. Start by writing a number on the driveway with the chalk, such as the number three. Tell your child, "You are starting with three points. Let's see if you can add two more points by making a basket." Your child then tosses the ball into the box. If he makes it, you yell, "Two points!" You say to your child, "You started with three points; you scored two more points. How many points do you have all together?" Your child will answer five. As you say this to your child, you write the math equation on the driveway with the chalk: $3+2=5$. If necessary, draw tally lines under the numbers so your child can count them using one-to-one correspondence or he may use his fingers to figure out the problem. If your child misses the basket, the equation becomes $3+0=3$.

Variations:

- Make each basket worth one point or three points.
- For an indoor game, use masking tape for the line and paper and markers to write the equation.

Zigzag

Materials:

- six medium-sized boxes or buckets
- six golf balls
- a bucket with a handle or a child's pail
- measuring tape

Your child is counting on as she zigzags across the yard.

Directions

Set up two rows of three boxes each. Make the rows five feet (1.5 m) apart and place the boxes four feet (1.2 m) from each other. Do not line the two rows of boxes up across from each other, but rather kitty-corner to make a zigzag pattern. Place the six golf balls in the bucket with the handle. Your child will use these golf balls to count on from a given number. Have your child stand at one end of the rows. You call out a number, such as four. Your child runs and drops a golf ball into the first box. As she does, she calls out the number five. She then runs kitty-corner to the first box in the opposite row, drops in a golf ball, and calls out "six." She continues until all of her golf balls are in the boxes. She then collects the golf balls, returns to her starting position, and waits for you to call out another starting number.

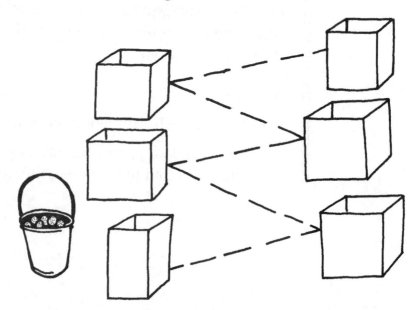

Mother, May I?

Materials:

• none

This variation on an old time favorite will have your child counting his way across the yard.

Directions

Have your child stand on one side of the yard. You stand about 25 feet (7.7 m) away on the other side of the yard. Face each other. You start by calling out, for example, "You may take three giant steps." Your child answers, "Mother, may I?" You answer, "Yes, you may." And then your child takes three steps as big as he can. Make sure he counts the steps out loud. Let's say you call out, "You may take seven tiny steps." Your child answers with, "Mother, may I?" You say, "Yes, you may." Your child must wait for the verbal exchange before he takes his steps or he must return to where he started and begin again. Continue this process until your child gets close enough to touch you. When he does, he wins.

Variations:

• Use different step descriptions, such as, huge, large, gigantic, long, miniature, baby, small, minute, or short.

• Use animal descriptions for steps, such as, elephant, monkey, giraffe, alligator, polar bear, ant, worm, turtle, rabbit, penguin, seal, or grasshopper.

• Can be played indoors.

From Here to There

Materials:

• none

Your child adds and subtracts to get from one end of the yard to the other.

Directions

Have your child stand on one side of the yard. You stand on the other. Tell your child that her goal is to hop across the yard to you. But there is a catch. She can only hop towards you when you say, "add," and she must hop backwards (away from you) when you say, "subtract." For instance, you say, "add three." Your child hops forward three times. You say, "subtract one" and she hops backward one time. Continue adding and subtracting until your child reaches you on the other side of the yard.

Variations:

- Use the words "plus," "minus," and "take-away."

- Paint a plus (+) sign on one side of a large piece of cardboard and a minus (-) sign on the other. When you say add or plus, show the plus (+) side of the cardboard. When you say "take-away," "minus," or "subtract," show the minus (-) side of the cardboard.

- Can be played as an indoor game.

Squeal Deal

Materials:

- balloons
- chalk

As his balloon squeals across the yard, your child learns to measure distance by his foot.

Directions

Draw a chalk starting line on the driveway. Have your child stand behind the line. Stretch out the balloon for him and have him blow it up (if he can). Then your child lets the balloon go. Have your child count the number of "feet" away from the chalk line that the balloon landed. He measures the "feet" by stepping off each heel-to-toe step with his own foot. Have him retrieve the balloon and try to better his distance.

Variations:

- Get a different colored balloon for yourself and join in the game.

- Have your child estimate the distance before he measures it.

- Can be played as an indoor game.

Bucket Brigade

Materials:

- play pool
- different sized containers (ice cream buckets, whipped topping containers, margarine tubs, sand pails, square food storage containers, or water jugs)
- an eight-ounce (240 ml) liquid measuring cup

Learning to measure becomes one big splash.

Directions

Fill the pool with water. Gather the containers together. Next, give your child the liquid measuring cup. Then have her fill the empty containers with water using the measuring cup. Have her count each cup as she pours it into the various containers. How many cups does it take to fill each container? Which container holds the most water? Which holds the least? Be sure to do a lot of splashing!

Variations:

- Before filling an empty container, have your child estimate the number of cups she thinks it will hold.
- As an indoor game, play in the bathtub.

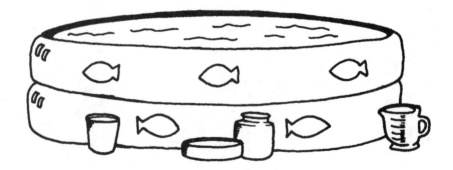

Splish, Splash, Make It Fast!

Materials:

- play pool
- plastic lids from margarine containers
- permanent markers
- bucket

A hot afternoon, a cool pool, and lots of learning are what your child will have.

Directions

On the plastic lids, as large as you can, write the letters of the alphabet with a permanent marker. Then fill your child's pool and place the covers randomly in the pool. Set the bucket next to the pool so your child can reach it without getting out of the pool. Once your child is in the pool, say, "Splish, splash, make it fast! Find the letter Z." Your child then, as quickly as she can, finds the letter Z and puts it into the bucket. As she places the letter into the bucket, have her say the letter name.

Variations:

- Use letter sounds.
- Use colors.
- Use shapes.
- Use numbers.
- Use uppercase and lowercase letters and have your child find the matches as quickly as possible.
- As an indoor game, play at bath time.

Animal Freeze

Materials:

• a sprinkler

A sprinkling shower is a good way to cool off on a hot day.

Directions

Set up your sprinkler in a place that needs a little water. Have your child don his bathing suit and tell him the following rules. He will run around the sprinkler (that is turned off) until you turn on the water. Then he must freeze. He cannot move until you call out an animal name and he plays out the part with actions and sounds. All the while, he is being sprinkled by water. When he completes his actions, he may run out of the water. Then you turn the water off and the game starts all over again.

Possible Creatures to Act Out:

• cat, dog, mouse, lion, tiger, elephant, bee, butterfly, rabbit, frog, snake, worm, snail, ant, giraffe, spider, chicken, rooster, hawk, eagle, robin, fly, horse, cow, pig, monkey, ape, cheetah, caterpillar, bat, donkey, lamb, alligator, seal, clam, ostrich, flamingo, turtle

Variations:

• Have your child do transportation actions (running, walking, hopping or skipping).

• Call out a number and have him hop that many times before he can escape from the water.

• Call out a letter and have your child run around the sprinkler once as he repeats its sound.

ABC Slalom

Materials:

- chalk
- yardstick

He hops to the left; he hops to the right. He skis on the giant slalom as he learns his alphabet.

Directions

Write a large uppercase "A" ten inches (25 cm) tall. Write the uppercase letter "B" six inches (15 cm) above the "A," and slightly to the right. Then write the uppercase letter "C" six inches (15 cm) above the "B," and slightly to the left. You will be creating a zigzag effect with the letters of the alphabet. Your child will then slalom the letters. He does this by hopping onto the letter "A" with both feet and calling out the letter name. He hops to the "B" and calls out the letter name. Then it's off to the "C." He continues this zigzag pattern for the entire alphabet.

Variations:

- Create the zigzag slalom using different shapes.
- Create the slalom using the lowercase letters of the alphabet.
- Create the slalom using numbers.
- Use just the short vowels—a, e, i, o, u—and have your child call out the sound of the letter as he hops on it. You can do this with any of the letter sounds.

Language Ladder

Materials:

- chalk
- yardstick

Stepping up the ladder, your child learns adjectives for big and small.

Directions

Draw the two sides of the ladder two feet (61 cm) apart. Draw short perpendicular lines connecting the two sides. These are the rungs of the ladder. Have your child "climb" the ladder by stepping on each rung. Identify the "kind" of step your child is taking—little or big—by having her say it aloud as she steps. Draw the step lines very close together for little (small, tiny, itsy-bitsy, teeny-weeny, short, miniature, puny, dinky, minute, microscopic) steps. Draw the step lines very far apart for big (enormous, huge, gigantic, colossal, gargantuan, large, grand, great, long, mammoth, astronomical, expansive, tremendous) steps. This is a great way to learn adjectives.

Variations:

- Make the rungs of the ladder in a color pattern (red, white, blue, red, white, blue, etc.). Have your child only step on one certain color as she climbs the ladder.

- Have your child count the number of rungs on the ladder.

Sound Boxes

Materials:

- chalk
- yardstick

Your child will soon be marching his way to knowing his beginning letter sounds.

Directions

Randomly draw eight ten-inch (25 cm) squares over a chosen area. Write an uppercase letter in each box. Call out a letter and have your child run to it. Once he is there ask, "What's the letter? What's the sound?" He tells you and then lists words that begin with that sound. As he lists the words, he will be marching in place. When he can think of no more words, he stops marching. For example, you call out the letter "B." Your child runs to the "B" box. He tells you the letter is "B" and the sound is /b/. He starts marching and listing words that start with the /b/ sound: ball, boy, box, block, Bob, bean, bear. If your child has difficulty identifying beginning sound words, say the words first and have him repeat them. He stops marching when he runs out of "B" words. Call out another letter and repeat the process.

Variations:

- Use small letters.
- Use two-letter blends (sh, ch, wh, th)

Action Boxes

Materials:

- chalk
- yardstick

The letter is J. The sound is /j/. And your child jumps, jumps, jumps.

Directions

Draw ten 12-inch (30 cm) boxes in a row. Put an uppercase letter in each box. Start at one end of the row. When your child jumps into that box, she must say the letter and its sound. Next, she must do an action that starts with that letter. She may need some help with the actions. When she finishes the action, she jumps to the next box and repeats the steps with the new letter.

Possible Action Words:

- **A**: answer, add, announce
- **B**: bite, blow, bow, blink, bob, bounce, bend, brush
- **C**: curtsy, crouch, cough, cry, climb, crawl, cut, clap
- **D**: dig, duck, drive, dance, drink, dip, dribble, dust
- **E**: eat, exhale
- **F**: freeze, flop, fly, frown, fidget, flip, fish, fall
- **G**: giggle, grin, gobble, gallop, grunt, grow, growl
- **H**: hop, hiss, hide, hug, hum, howl, hiccup
- **I**: imitate
- **J**: jiggle, jump, jerk, juggle
- **K**: kick, kiss
- **L**: lick, leap, look, listen, love, lean, limp
- **M**: move, march, mumble, measure, mop, moan, munch

- **N**: nibble, nod, nudge
- **O**: open, order
- **P**: pucker, pedal, pat, pinch, pitch, pound, point, pour
- **Q**: quit
- **R**: run, ride, rip, roar, reach, rock, roll, rotate
- **S**: smile, sit, squat, salute, sway, swim, sweep scream, sleep, skip, stomp, stretch, sneeze, snort, scratch
- **T**: turn, twirl, twist, throw, think, thump, touch, tuck
- **U**: uncover
- **V**: vacuum
- **W**: wiggle, wave, wind, walk, waddle, wipe, wash, whine,
- **Y**: yodel, yank, yell
- **Z**: zigzag, zoom, zip

Capital Shuffle

Materials:

- chalk
- measuring tape

The faster the better when matching uppercase and lowercase letters.

Directions

Draw two parallel lines, eight feet (2.4 m) apart and ten feet (2.5 m) in length. Along the outside of one line, write ten uppercase letters with the base of the letters on the line. On the outside of the opposite line, write the same letters in their lowercase form but in a different order. Draw a square in the center between the two lines. Have your child stand in the square. Call out, "On your mark, get set, find the uppercase letter D." Your child runs to the letter and hops on it. Then tell him to find the lowercase letter d. He runs and hops on the lowercase letter d and returns to the center square. Start again with another letter.

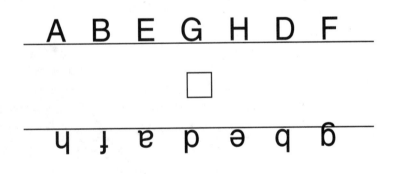

Variation:

- Use big shapes and small shapes.

Tightrope Walking

Materials:

• chalk

Your child does a balancing act as he walks along these lines.

Directions

Draw a chalk line. Draw it straight, wavy, or curly. Have your child walk on it as if he was a tightrope walker— hands and arms straight out from his sides for balance and pointing his toes with each step.

Variations:

- Change the type of step your child uses to walk the tightrope: heel-to-toe, tiptoe, giant steps, skip, sashay, or backwards.

- Create a pattern of steps your child must use to walk the tightrope: three heel-to-toe steps, three giant steps, three tiptoe steps, and then repeat the pattern.

Big, Bigger, Biggest

Materials:

- chalk
- yardstick

The concept of comparing objects as big, bigger, and biggest is made easy as your child jumps through this activity.

Directions

Draw a one-foot (30 cm) square. Draw a two-foot (61 cm) square next to it. Draw a three-foot (91 cm) square next to the second square. Ask your child, "If this square is big (pointing to the first square), what can you tell me about this square (pointing to the second square)?" He should answer, "It is bigger." Then ask your child, "If the first square is big, and the second square is bigger than the first square, what can you tell me about the last square?" He should answer, "It is the biggest." Have your child jump onto the first square and shout out "big." Have him jump to the next square and shout "bigger." Then have your child jump into the third square and shout "biggest." Draw another set of the three squares, but draw them in a random order. Then have your child identify the big, bigger, and biggest squares.

1 Foot

2 Feet

3 Feet

Variations:

- Use different shapes and call out the shape name as well as the size (big circle, bigger circle, biggest circle).

- Adapt the game and do wide, wider, widest.

- Create pictures that are silly, sillier, and silliest.

Small, Smaller, Smallest

Materials:

- chalk
- yardstick

Your child will understand small, smaller, and smallest as she sees objects shrink in size.

Directions

Draw a one-foot (30 cm) square. Draw a six-inch (15 cm) square next to it. Draw a three-inch (8 cm) square next to the second square. Ask your child, "If this square (pointing to the first square) is small, what can you tell me about this square (pointing to the second square)?" She should answer, "It is smaller." Then ask your child, "If the first square is small and the second square is smaller than the first square, what can you tell me about the last square?" She should answer, "It is the smallest." Have your child jump into the first square and shout "small." Have her jump into the second square and shout "smaller." Then have your child jump onto the third square and shout "smallest." Draw another set of the three squares, but draw them in a random order. Then have your child identify the squares in order—small, smaller, smallest.

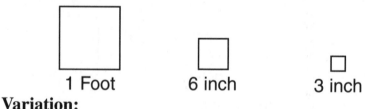

1 Foot   6 inch   3 inch

Variation:

- Use different shapes and call out the shape name as well as the size (small triangle, smaller triangle, smallest triangle).

House of Prepositions

Materials:

- chalk
- measuring tape

With this house, your child will begin to understand many of the prepositional phrases he hears each day.

Directions

Draw a simple house five feet (1.5 m) tall. Be sure to have a roof, a door, two second story windows, and a curved walkway leading up to the door. To the left of the house, add two bushes with some space between them. Then add a tall tree to the right of the house. Direct your child to stand in certain areas or perform certain actions by using prepositional phrases (phrases that include directional words).

Possible Phrases:

Stand . . .
- between the windows
- at the door
- on the roof
- beside the tree
- above the house
- among the bushes
- near the house
- by the walkway
- in the tree
- before the door
- upon the walkway

Walk . . .
- across the walkway
- toward the house
- along the walkway
- beyond the house
- around the tree
- through the bushes

Common Prepositions (directional words):

- in, on, between, over, under, behind, through, beside, by, against, near, to, above, across, after, around, below, into, off, past, toward(s), underneath, up, upon, within, along, among, at, before, beyond, down, in back of, instead of

Swirl-and-Whirl

Materials:

- chalk
- yardstick

Watch out for a dizzy kid when your child follows a spiral path to learning her alphabet.

Directions

Draw a spiral figure that looks like a snail shell. Your starting point will be the very center. Start by drawing a letter "C" one foot (30 cm) tall. Continue with your line as if to circle the "C," but keep your line a distance of one foot (30 cm) away from your previous line. Continue circling until you have created three swirls around the center "C." Next, draw straight lines across the path the swirls have made, thereby creating 26 blocks. Write an uppercase letter in each block. Start with the letter "A" in the first block on the outside.

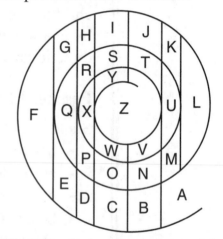

The center circle will be "Z." Have your child start with "A" and sing the alphabet song as she steps on each letter.

Variations:

- Use lowercase letters.
- Use numbers, shapes, or colors.

Water Printing

Materials:

- a bucket of water
- a two-inch (5 cm) wide paintbrush

Kids and water are always a great combination. Add the letters of the alphabet, and your child will have hours of fun.

Directions

Fill the bucket with water. Give your child an old paint brush. Find a sidewalk or driveway. Starting at one end of the sidewalk or driveway, have your child start painting the alphabet. Challenge him to try to finish all 26 letters before they dry and fade away.

Variations:

- Have your child print his name.
- List numbers.
- Create shapes.
- Paint solid shapes and outlines.

Stone Steppin'

Materials:

• chalk

The letters of the alphabet are your child's stepping stones as she makes her way across this stream.

Directions

Your driveway is the perfect stream for your child to cross. You will be creating a "path" of letters for her to use as stepping stones to cross over the river. Choose a letter such as "b." Start on one side of the driveway and write the letters within stepping distance of the edge. Repeat the letter "b" in a random path all the way across the driveway. Then pick another letter and do the same. Be sure to intertwine the letters and not to spread them too far apart. It may be enough to start with four or five different letters. Have your child begin on the edge of the stream where you started writing the letters, so she will be looking at the letters right side up. Let's say you call out the letter "b." Your child crosses the stream by stepping only on that letter until she gets to the other side of the driveway. Have her return to her starting position and then you call out another letter.

Variations:

• Create a path of shapes.
• Create a path of numbers.

Bucket Ball

Materials:

- five buckets
- a tennis ball
- paper
- marker
- masking tape
- scissors
- measuring tape
- chalk

A toss of the ball into a bucket makes quick learning of short vowels.

Directions

Cut five four-inch (10 cm) squares from the paper. Write the vowels, **a**, **e**, **i**, **o**, and **u**, in lowercase letters on the paper. Tape them to the five buckets. Draw an X on the driveway with the chalk and set the five buckets in a circle around the center X. Place the buckets four feet (1 m) from the X. Have your child stand on the X and toss the tennis ball into the bucket. When it goes in, she runs around the outside of the circle of buckets chanting that short vowel sound until she reaches that short vowel bucket. She grabs the ball out of the bucket and returns to the center X. She then tries to toss the ball into the next bucket.

Variations:

- Tell your child the sound. She must find the bucket to toss the ball into.
- Use any letters of the alphabet.
- As an indoor game, use a rolled-up sock for your ball.

A Circus Performance

Materials:

- chalk, hula-hoops, or jump ropes
- measuring tape

What a circus you will have in your driveway when, in ring number one, your child becomes a ferocious tiger.

Directions

In your driveway, draw three five-foot (1.5 m) circles in a straight row one foot (30 cm) apart. They will be the rings of your circus. You can also use hula-hoops or jump ropes for the circles. Inform your child that the circle on the left is the "first" ring, the circle in the middle is the "second" ring, and the circle on the right is the "last" ring. Then begin the show. Say, "Ladies and gentlemen, I welcome you to the greatest circus on Earth! In the first ring . . . ." Your child runs and stands in the first circle. Then say, ". . . we have a ferocious tiger." Your child sounds and acts like a tiger. Then continue with another circle, "In the last ring we have a powerful elephant." Your child runs to the third circle and acts like an elephant. Use the words first, second, last, third, middle, ring number one, ring number two, and ring number three. Keep him hopping from ring to ring.

Possible Acts to Perform:

- tigers, elephants, horses, monkeys, jugglers, flame eaters, tightrope walkers, happy clowns, sad clowns, clowns with big feet, acrobats, dogs, magicians, man being shot from a cannon, trapeze artists

Variation:

- As an indoor game, use masking tape for the circles.

To the Top

Materials:

- chalk
- yardstick

Climbing a pyramid of letters becomes your child's path to learning the alphabet and the sounds those letters make.

Directions

Create a pyramid of 26 one-foot (30-cm) squares. Start by drawing a row of six squares that are connected together. Then center a row of five squares on top of the first row. Continue with another row of five squares and then a row of four. Next, add a row of three, a row of two, and finally one square on the top of the pyramid. You will have seven rows and a total of 26 squares. Starting in the lower left-hand square of the pyramid, write the letter A and continue in alphabetical order to the right until you reach the letter F. Then move to the square in the row above the letter F. It will be the far right-hand square in the second row. Start with the letter G and continue to the left alphabetically through K. Continue this process until you reach the letter Z in the top square. Have your child start with the letter A. She must hop into the square, say the letter, and then tell you the sound the letter makes. She then jumps into the B box and repeats the process. If she misses a letter or sound, she must go to the beginning and start again.

Variations:

- Have your child sing the alphabet song as she hops through the squares.
- Have your child just say the sounds of the letters.
- Create a pyramid of numbers, shapes, or colors.
- As an indoor game, use masking tape to create the pyramid.

Category Hop

Materials:

- chalk
- yardstick

Naming objects that belong in the group will make your child a winner.

Directions

On the driveway create a row of six connected 18-inch (46 cm) squares. In each box, write a category such as colors, fruits, animals, letters, friends, and shapes. Then have your child start at one end of the row. Tell him that the magic number is "three" and that in each box he must name three things that belong in that group. As he hops into the first square, you tell him the name of the category in that box, such as fruits. Your child must list three fruits and he must hop as he names each one. When he has named all three, he then hops into the next box, you give him another category and he plays again.

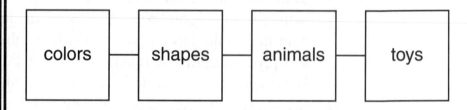

Possible Categories:

- numbers, colors, fruits, vegetables, farm animals, sea animals, animals that fly, insects, letters, friends, relatives, shapes, things in the bedroom, things we eat, instruments, television shows, songs, stuffed animals, toys, games, things in a house, things on a car, books, or places we go

Here We Go 'Round

Materials:

- a tree or bush

A twist on an old favorite has your child going 'round and 'round.

Directions

Find a bush or tree that you and your child can walk around with no interference. Start singing these words to the tune of the song, "Here We Go 'Round the Mulberry Bush":

> *"Here we walk 'round the mulberry bush, mulberry bush, mulberry bush.*
>
> *Here we walk 'round the mulberry bush so early in the morning."*

Then change the walk to run, skip, hop, gallop, walk backwards, tiptoe, march, crawl, jump, float, fly, flap, swim, meander, twirl, glide, slither, slide, leap, swirl, buzz, creep, or sashay, and continue the game.

Need music? Try *Wee Sing* by Pamela Conn Beall and Susan Hagen Nipp, published in 1985 by Price Stern Sloan of Los Angeles.

Magic Letter Wand

Materials:

- a ruler, stick, or wand

Beginning sounds are magically learned.

Directions

Use a ruler or stick that is one foot (30 cm) long as a magic wand. If you wish, you and your child can decorate the wand with ribbons before you start the game. Begin the game by waving the wand over your child and saying, "Abracadabra, the magic letter is T." Your child must tell you the sound that the letter makes. Again wave the wand and say, "The magic letter is T, and you are a turkey." Your child begins moving around the yard acting like a turkey. Then change your child's actions with a wave of the wand and she becomes a turtle, a trumpet, a tambourine, or even a tornado as long as the object begins with a T. Wave your wand to change the letter and start all over again. This game can be played indoors, too.

Box It

Materials:

- many different sized boxes
- different colored construction paper
- scissors
- glue

An array of boxes helps your child get a jump on colors.

Directions

Gather together boxes of different sizes and shapes. You can use shoeboxes, jewelry boxes, packing boxes, and even boxes big enough to crawl through. Assign each box a color by gluing a piece of colored construction paper to each side (or you and your child can paint each box). Have your child distribute the boxes in your yard, then give him different directions that relate to the boxes and their colors.

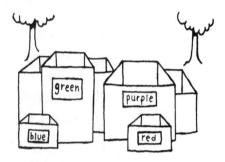

Possible Directions:

- Run and touch all the green boxes.
- Run around each of the blue boxes.
- Jump over all the red boxes.
- Toss all the yellow boxes in the air.
- Put all the orange boxes in a pile.
- Stack the pink boxes.
- Skip to all the black boxes.
- Lift all the brown boxes.
- Line up all the white boxes.
- Create color patterns using the boxes.

Match It

Materials:

- chalk
- yardstick

As your child puts each foot on a matching shape, she not only learns her shapes but her pairs, too.

Directions

Draw a two-foot square (61 cm). Make it into a four by four grid resulting in 16 squares. Using eight different shapes—square, circle, rectangle, triangle, oval, diamond, heart, and star— randomly draw a shape in each box. You will use each shape twice. Then have your child find the pairs. Tell her to find the hearts. She puts one foot on a heart and finds another heart with her other foot. Or if she finds it easier, she can put 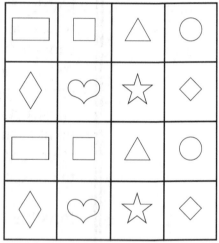 her hand in one box and her feet in another box to find the matching pair. Make sure she names the pair of shapes. She can say, "I found a pair of hearts."

Variations:

- Use colors.
- Use uppercase and lowercase letters as matches.

Hippity-Hop, Find the Spot

Materials:

- chalk
- measuring tape

Fast paced and fun, your child will run in circles learning his colors and shapes.

Directions

Draw a large circle 12 feet (3 m) in diameter. Around the outside perimeter of the circle, draw different colored shapes 10 inches (25 cm) apart. Repeat shapes as many times as needed to complete the circle, but make sure repeated shapes are different colors. No two shapes should be exactly the same. Have your child start in the center of the circle. Then say, "Hippity-hop, find the spot with the red square." Your child must then run to the named shape and hop on it. Call out another colored shape, and your child hippity-hops around the circle to find it.

Variations:

- Use letters, either uppercase or lowercase.
- Use numbers or number sets.

Pick a Pair

Materials:

- chalk
- measuring tape

Matching pairs is as easy as picking apples in this game.

Directions

Draw the outline of a tree with the top measuring a five-foot area (1.5 m). Inside the tree, draw the shapes of fruit. Make sure you have two (a pair) of each type of fruit that are the same color. Have your child stand on the trunk. Call out, "Find a pair of green apples." She runs to one of the apples, jumps on it and counts off "one." Then she runs to the other apple and counts off "two." End by saying, "You found the pair of green apples." Have your child return to the trunk and start over finding another pair.

Suggested Pairs of Fruits:

- green apples, red apples, yellow bananas, green pears, red cherries, yellow lemons, green limes, orange oranges, orange peaches, purple grapes

Variations:

- Create a shape tree.
- Create an alphabet tree.
- Create a number tree.

Somewhere Over That Rainbow

Materials:

- chalk
- measuring tape

As your child travels over this rainbow, he will be finding more than just the color gold.

Directions

Draw a five-foot (1.5 m) rainbow, using four different colors for the arches. On the right side of the rainbow, draw objects using the four colors of that rainbow. For example, if the rainbow colors are red, yellow, green, and purple, the objects drawn may be an apple, a heart, a banana, a sun, a leaf, a frog, grapes, and a flower. Have your child start on the left side of the rainbow. Call out, "Somewhere over that rainbow we are looking for something . . . red." He then tightrope walks (skips, runs, hops, gallops, tiptoe, or heel-toe walks) along the red arch of the rainbow. When he reaches the end of the rainbow, he must run to an object that is red. Be sure he states what he has found. Have your child return to the left side of the rainbow and choose another color to follow.

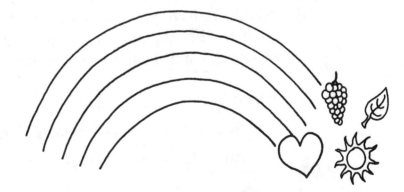

Please Note: Starting at the top of the rainbow, the true colors are red, orange, yellow, green, blue, indigo, and violet.

The House That I Built

Materials:

- chalk
- tape measure

Your child's house takes shape as you build a house of squares and triangles.

Directions

Tell your child that she is going to build a house using different shapes such as squares, rectangles, triangles, circles. Ask your child if she wants her house to be a square or a rectangle. Draw the base of the house large—about five feet (1.5 m). Ask her

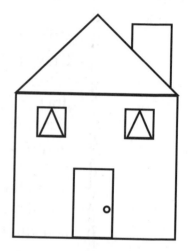

questions about different parts of the house and what shapes they should be: roof (triangle), chimney (rectangle), windows (squares), curtains (triangles), door (rectangle), doorknob (circle). Make sure that every part of the house that is drawn is a shape. When the house has been built, have your child identify the shapes by hopping on them. For example, tell your child to, "Find a rectangle," and she must run over and hop on the door.

Variations:

- Add trees and a garden using shapes.
- Add a family using shapes.

Rope Work

Materials:

- jump rope or six-foot (1.8 m) piece of rope

A rope in your child's hands is the beginning of his unlimited imagination.

Directions

Using the jump rope or piece of rope, create different shapes. The driveway or sidewalk works best because it is flat. Make a circle, square, oval, triangle, rectangle, and heart. Be sure to discuss the different characteristics of each shape.

Variations:

- Create different kinds of lines such as straight, curvy, jagged, long, short, and wavy.
- Create numbers out of the rope.
- Create letters out of the rope.
- As an indoor game, you can use yarn.

Safety Note: Always supervise your child when he is using jump ropes.

Red Rover

Materials:

- outside toys or objects of many different colors

A twist on an old favorite will have your child recognizing his colors.

Directions

Set up your backyard so that you and your child are standing on one side of your yard and all of the different colored toys are lined up on the other side. Call out the old chant, "Red Rover, Red Rover, send green right over." Your child then runs to the other side of the yard and grabs a green toy. He returns to your side of the yard with his prize, and you call out the chant asking for another color. You can play this indoors, too.

Possible Objects:

- balls, croquet balls, pails, shovels, flying discs, rocks, water pistols, garden gloves, painted boxes, a baseball glove, tricycle (he'll have to ride it), hats, mittens, scarves, blocks, shoes, silverware

Triangle Trip

Materials:

- yarn
- trees, swing set, deck, clothesline pole, anything yarn can be tied to drawings or cardboard cutouts of different shaped triangles

Understanding that a triangle has three points and three sides will become an easy task.

Directions

Show your child the drawings of the different triangles. Discuss the similarities of the shapes (three points, three sides, three angles). Be sure to mention that the prefix "tri" is used to indicate three of something. You might mention to your child that her tricycle has three wheels. Next, tell your child that she is going to be making her own triangle in her backyard. Tell her that it doesn't matter what her triangle looks like as long as it has the criteria that make up a triangle (three points, three sides, three angles). Have your child pick three points in your backyard. They can be a tree, a swing set pole, or even a chair leg. Next, have your child tie one end of the yarn to the first point in the triangle. Then have her run the yarn to the next point and wrap it around that point and continue on until she reaches the point where she started. Tie the yarn. Review the attributes of a triangle again, and then have your child run along the sides of the triangle she just made.

Rock Put

Materials:

- chalk
- rock
- measuring tape

A toss of a stone and your child learns shapes and colors.

Directions

Make a circle 10 feet (3 m) in diameter. In the center of the circle, make a one-foot (30-cm) square. Outside the perimeter of the circle, draw different shapes of different colors. Draw at least eight shapes. No two shapes should be exactly the same. Then have your child stand in the center square. Tell him he must remain inside the square. Next, call out a colored shape such as "blue circle," for example. Your child must then "put" or toss the rock into the blue circle. He then retrieves the rock and returns to his starting place in the square. Continue by calling out another colored shape.

Variations:

- Use letters.
- Use numbers.

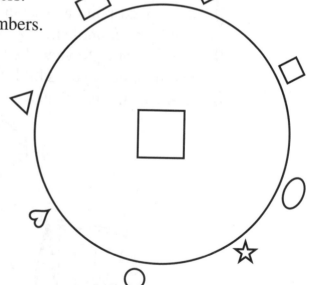

All Boxed Up

Materials:

- many different sized boxes (shoeboxes, jewelry boxes, packing boxes, etc.)
- different colored construction paper
- scissors
- glue

There are boxes that are big and boxes that are small. Your child will learn them all.

Directions

Gather boxes of different sizes and shapes. Assign each box a color by gluing a piece of colored construction paper to each side (or you and your child can paint each box). In your yard, have your child randomly distribute the boxes. Then give her different directions that relate to the boxes and their sizes. You can play this game indoors, too.

Possible Directions:

- Line up all the boxes from smallest to largest.
- Line up the red boxes from biggest to smallest.
- Make a group of small boxes and a group of big boxes.
- Put the boxes in a row starting with a small box, then a big box, then a small box, etc.
- Stack all the big boxes.
- Put the small boxes in a pile.
- Build one big box using all of the boxes.
- Separate the boxes into a small box pile, a medium box pile, and a large box pile.
- Make a caterpillar with the boxes.

Hoops

Materials:

- hula-hoop

You'll have your child jumping through hoops in no time.

Directions

Your child will basically be following different directions on what to do with his hula hoop. Start by having him place his hoop on the ground. Then give him the directions. This game can be played indoors, too.

Possible Directions:

- Jump inside the hoop.

- Run (skip, hop, jog, gallop) around the outside of the hoop.

- Jump over the hoop.

- Act like a frog (bunny, horse, dog, cat, bee, spider, lion, elephant, butterfly, ant, fish, eagle, cow, chicken, octopus, snail, snake) inside the hoop.

- Hold the hula-hoop in a vertical position and give your child the following directions: jump (hop, crawl, skip, jog, gallop, swagger) through the hoop, go through the hoop backwards, go through the hoop head (feet, right foot, left foot, right arm, left arm, knees, backside, elbows, fingers, toes, nose) first, act like a rabbit (hippo, caterpillar, or any other creature) going through the hoop, be a train (car, truck, boat, plane, helicopter, bus) going through the hoop.

Variation:

- Let your child think of his own ways to go through the hoop.

Hopping Down the Bunny Trail

Materials:

- boxes of different sizes
- one large box big enough to crawl through
- three boxes small enough to hop over
- a slide
- a six feet (1.8 m) long two by four inch (5 cm x 10 cm) board
- measuring tape

It's a race, and your child is always the winner on this obstacle course.

Directions

In different areas around your backyard, you will be setting up activities. Your child will be doing these activities in a specified sequence. Choose an area and set up a line of three boxes that your child can hop over. Five feet (1.5 m) away set up a large box that your child can crawl through. Next, your child can climb up the slide and slide down. She can then run to another row of six boxes that she weaves through. She does a forward roll and walks across the two by four inch (5 cm x 10 cm) balance beam that is laying flat on the ground. When she completes the activities, she wins.

Variation:

- Use any outdoor games to create your own obstacle course.

Apart . . . Together

Materials:

- chalk
- yardstick

These slow-motion jumping jacks encourage your child's coordination for the real thing.

Directions

Draw two 10-inch (25 cm) circles a shoulder width apart. Then center a single 10-inch (25 cm) circle above the two circles in pyramid style, but not touching. Repeat the pattern four more times. Have your child start with his feet "apart" in the two circles. Call out "together" as he jumps into the single circle with feet together. Repeat calling out, "apart . . . together," as your child jumps through the circles.

Variation:

- Include the arms. In the "apart" position have your child hold arms straight out from his body at shoulder height. For the "together" position, have him clap his hands together over his head.

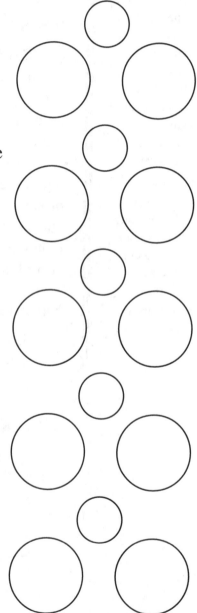

Off to the Races

Materials:

- chalk
- measuring tape

Of course, there is never a loser in this race of learning.

Directions

Create two (or more) race tracks that run parallel to each other. Make them approximately 25 feet (7.7 m) long and 2 feet (61 cm) wide. Create a starting line and a finish line. Have your child stand behind the starting line of one of the racetracks and a friend (or yourself) behind the other. Count down by saying, "On your mark, get set, go!" The children then race to the finish line where they are crowned "first winner" and "second winner."

Variations:

- Use different racing modes such as running, hopping, skipping, galloping, taking giant steps, running backwards, heel-toe stepping, hopping on one foot, tiptoeing, moving with animal actions.

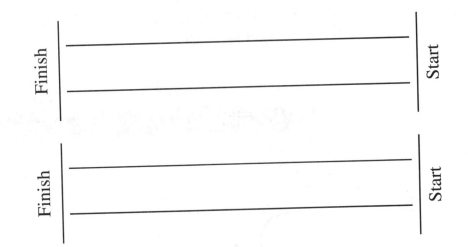

Marching Feet

Materials:

- chalk
- feet

Marching along in "foot prints" will teach your child her left and right.

Directions

Trace your child's left foot and then her right foot (or you may trace your own feet). Trace five of each foot. You can use different ways to help your child identify left and right. Use one color for the left foot and another for the right. You can write an "L" in the left foot and an "R" in the right or you can spell the word in each foot. Have your child say "left" and "right" as she marches along the path.

Variations:

- After several steps, increase or decrease the distance between each step to add variety.

- Change the speed at which your child marches.

- Teach hopping on one foot by drawing several left or right steps in a row.

People Parts

Materials:

- chalk
- mirror

Not only does your child learn to identify her eyes and ears, she also learns descriptive details about herself.

Directions

Have your child lie on the sidewalk. Trace her body. Discuss details about each body part before your child draws it: Where should you draw your hair? What color is your hair? Is your hair long or short? Is your hair straight or curly? Do you have bangs? Where are your eyes? How many eyes do you have? What color are your eyes? What are the little hairs around your eyes called? Have your child look at herself in a mirror to identify some of her facial details. Continue on with the rest of her body parts.

Variations:

- Use only the face.
- As an indoor game, use newsprint or butcher paper.

Truckin' Trikes

Materials:

- chalk
- tricycle or other riding toy
- yardstick

Your child will have hours of fun riding her tricycle along her very own road.

Directions

Draw two parallel lines 24 inches (61 cm) apart—big enough so your child's riding toy can be ridden between the lines. Make the lines the same color. Draw them straight or curvy. The road works best if it creates one continuous road so your child never has to stop and turn her tricycle around. Your driveway and sidewalks may naturally create a continuous road for your child to use. If it does not, you can create a "loop" where the road ends by drawing a "Y" and adding a "loop" that connects the top portion of the "Y," making it look like a huge bubble-blowing wand.

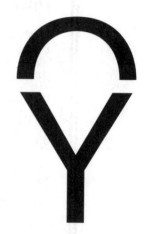

Variations:

- Draw large squares to represent places you frequently visit—grocery store, library, gas station, and the mall—so your child can drive to these places. Have your child get off of her tricycle and act out what happens at each stop.

- Draw stations (squares big enough for the child's tricycle) where your child can stop and play another game from this book.

Go West, Young Man

Materials:

- outside toys
- piece of cardboard two-feet (61 cm) square
- paint
- paintbrush
- measuring tape

Beginning map skills give your child great beginning direction.

Directions

On the piece of cardboard, paint a compass showing the directions of north, south, east, and west. Paint the letters—N, S, E, and W—to identify the directions. Lay your cardboard compass on the grass in your yard with the north arrow pointing north. Choose four toys. Place them ten feet (3 m) from your compass, straight out in each of the four directions. Have your child stand by the compass and identify the four directions. Then call out, "Go west, young man," and your child runs to the toy that is west, according to the compass, grabs it and places it on the "W" on the compass. Do this for all four directions. Replace the toys and start again.

Variation:

- Add the intermediate directions of northeast, northwest, southeast, and southwest (NE, NW, SE, and SW).

Roping It

Materials:

- a jump rope or a six-foot (1.8 m) piece of rope

Your child will do more than just jump over this rope.

Directions

Place the rope in a straight line on the driveway. Have your child jump over it, then jump back again. Have her walk on it like a tightrope walker and then try walking sideways on it. Create a circle with the rope. Have your child jump inside the circle, then jump outside the circle. Tell her to run around the circle forward and then backwards. Have her run around the circle keeping one foot on the circle and one foot outside the circle. Then try it with one foot inside the circle. Have her run around the circle with both feet on the rope. Tell her to sit inside the circle. Have her place one foot inside and one foot outside the circle. Tell her to put her hands inside the circle and her feet outside the circle. Have her do any other creative action you can think of. You can play this game indoors, too.

Safety Note: Always supervise your child when she is playing around jump ropes.

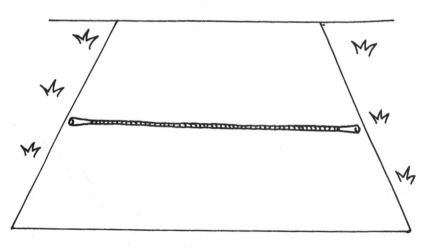

A Pile Here, a Pile There

Materials:

- piles of leaves
- a rake

Fall is fun as piles of leaves create an obstacle course.

Directions

Rake the leaves in your yard into piles. Make a row of five small piles three feet (1 m) apart. In another area of your yard, make two medium piles two feet (61 cm) apart. Then build a huge pile of leaves in yet another area of your yard. Establish a path for your child to run. For example, tell him that he is to zigzag through the five small piles, run between the two medium piles, and jump into the big pile of leaves. Count off numbers as he runs the course. Have him run the course again and try to beat his score. Then grab a rake and change the course.

Variations:

- Have your child do the course backwards.
- Have your child do the course while singing the alphabet song.

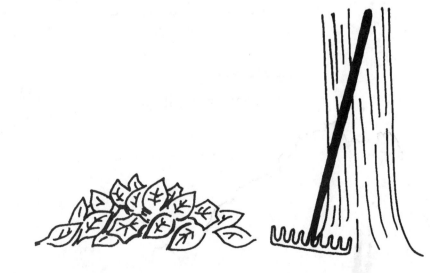

The Obstacle Course

Materials:

- chalk
- measuring tape

Your child will increase her coordination, build up her endurance, and learn to follow a series of directions as she has fun working her way through an obstacle course of her favorite games.

Directions

Choose three of the activities from the outdoor games section of this book and draw, or set them up, ten feet (3 m) apart on your sidewalk and driveway. Connect the different activities using, for example, "Tightrope Walking," "Language Ladder," or "Marching Feet." Have your child do the activities one after the other as quickly as she can. Be sure to cheer her on.

Variations:

- They are endless!

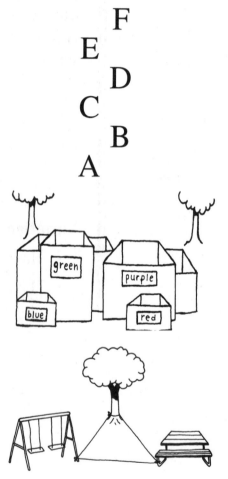

Homemade Chalk

Ingredients:

- one cup (240 ml) plaster of Paris (do not pack)
- one-half cup less two tablespoons (90 ml) cool water
- liquid tempera paint
- disposable container for mixing
- disposable stirring stick
- molds

Directions

Pour plaster of Paris into a disposable container. Stir in most of the water using a disposable stirring stick. Add three tablespoons (45 ml) of tempera paint. Mix well making sure the sediment at the bottom gets mixed in. Add the rest of the water in small increments so that the mixture thickens. Stir well and pour into the molds. Let the chalk dry. Remove from molds and have fun!

Things to Use as Molds:

- the fingers of old rubber gloves
- toilet tissue tubes with foil wrapped around the bottom
- paper cups
- margarine tubs
- plastic manicotti molds

Games/Skills Chart

Skill Category	Indoor Games	Outdoor Games
Addition	• Beanbag Equations • Clothespin Addition	• From Here to There • Number Line Addition • Two Points
Beginning Sounds	• Beginner's Box • Bop, Hop, Pop • Match Me • On My Trip to Jupiter . . .	• Action Boxes • Magic Letter Wand • Sound Boxes
Categorizing/ Grouping	• Find 10 • Group Hoops • Magazine I Spy • Paper Hearts • Station Stop • Special Square	• Category Hop
Color Recognition	• Blanket Board • Color Patrol • Memory • The Missing Egg • Paper Hearts • Tangled Up	• Box It • Hippity-Hop, Find the Spot • Pick a Pair • Red Rover • Rock Put • Somewhere Over That Rainbow
Counting Skills	• Beat, Beat, Beat, Went My Heart • Dot-to-Dot • Find 10 • Hallway Hop • Milky Way • Puddle Splashing • Sardines • Stair Steppin' • Teddy to Beddy • Time to Tally • Balloon Number Volley	• Bounce Once, Bounce Twice • Easy Catch • Falling Leaves • Hippity-Hop Hopscotch • Mighty Measures • Mother, May I? • Number Line Addition • Number Line Hip-Hop • Puddle Pond • One More, Please • Zigzag

Games/Skills Chart

Skill Category	Indoor Games	Outdoor Games
Creativity	• All Four on the Floor • Body Language • Creature Feature • Flight of the Bumblebee • Float, Flutter, Fly • Mirror, Mirror • Mommy's Mirror • Animal Crackers • Taped Tightrope	• A Circus Performance • Animal Freeze • Here We Go 'Round • Hoops • Magic Letter Wand • Rope Work • Roping It • Truckin' Trikes
Estimation	• Milky Way • Sardines	
Fine Motor Skills	• Button Up	
Following Directions	• All Four on the Floor • Body Patterns • Box Hop • Hands Up • Hokey Left and Pokey Right • Just One More • Mommy's Mirror • 1, 2, 3, Follow Me	• A Pile Here, a Pile There • All Boxed Up • Apart . . . Together • Box It • Hoops • Hopping Down the Bunny Trail • Mother, May I? • The Obstacle Course • Off to the Races
Fractions/ Graphing	• Big Bingo • Grid Work	• Parts of a Pie
Left and Right/ N, S, E, W	• Box Hop • Hokey Left and Pokey Right	• Go West, Young Man • Marching Feet
Letter Recognition	• A Fast Shuffle • Body Language • The Farmer Takes an "L" • The Race Is On • Tunnel Time	• ABC Slalom • Capital Shuffle • Sound Boxes • Splish, Splash, Make It Fast! • Stone Steppin' • Swirl-and-Whirl • To the Top • Water Printing

Games/Skills Chart

Skill Category	Indoor Games	Outdoor Games
Matching	• A Fast Shuffle • Behind Door #1 • Find My Match • Mitten Matching • Musical Matching Hearts • Shadow Shapes • Shape Box • Shape Up • Special Delivery • Tunnel Time	• Here's One, Find the Other • Match It • Pick a Pair
Measurement	• Straw Stretch	• Bucket Brigade • How Does Your Garden Grow? • Mighty Measures • Playing Footsy
Memory	• Just One More • On My Trip to Jupiter . . . • Memory • What's Your Number? • 1, 2, 3, Follow Me	
Money	• Money Pots	
Number Recognition	• Big Roller • The Race Is On • The Run Around	• Going Fishing • Hoppity Hop • Number Line Hip-Hop • One More, Please
Number Order	• Boxcars • Out of Order	• A Circus Performance • Number Line Hip-Hop